CARTER'S WAY

A No-Nonsense Method for Designing Your Own Super Stylish Home

Carter Oosterhouse

with Chris Peterson

Lyons Press
Guilford, Connecticut
An imprint of Globe Pequot Press

Lyons Press is an imprint of Globe Pequot Press.

Text design: Sheryl P. Kober
Project editors: Kristen Mellitt and Tracee Williams
Layout artist: Melissa Evarts

Library of Congress Cataloging-in-Publication Data

Oosterhouse, Carter.
  Carter's way : a no-nonsense method for designing your own super stylish home / Carter Oosterhouse.
       pages cm
  Summary: "Carter Oosterhouse, the popular host of HGTV's Carter Can, Million Dollar Rooms, and Red, Hot & Green, now offers homeowners a book featuring his simple, straightforward and super successful home-design process. He knows that home design can be intimidating, but his reassuring "you can do it" attitude encourages readers to use their imaginations and convinces them that they too can use his method to easily create beautiful living rooms, bedroom, kitchens, baths, and more!"— Provided by publisher.
  ISBN 978-0-7627-7898-0 (pbk.)
  1. Interior decoration. I. Peterson, Chris. II. Title.
  NK2115.O59 2012
  747—dc23
                                                                                    2012018144

Printed in the United States of America

10 9 8 7 6 5 4 3 2 1

CONTENTS

FOREWORD

Everything is possible. Anyone can cook. Give someone a bunch of ingredients, and 30 minutes later they have a meal. Carter feels the same way about homeowners. Give someone design basics, and a project is underway. With even the smallest tasks, Carter takes the same approach with homeowners that I do with cooks in the kitchen. His advice and designs are creative, helpful, attainable, and inspiring, AND he even calls the kitchen the hub of the house. That's my kind of guy!

I've turned to Carter numerous times on my daytime talk show, for help redesigning kitchens, offices, bathrooms, bedrooms, and beyond. You name it and he does it—WELL! His results always inspire the audience. I can't say I'm a DIY girl myself, but when Carter is on the show, he turns me into a believer and a doer. I've also had the pleasure of working with him on some of my most memorable shows and proudest moments to date. I've watched him passionately give back to communities—from renovating a culinary classroom at a high school in Philadelphia to redesigning a soup kitchen in Wilmington, Ohio, so more hungry people could get a warm meal and a little dignity. Through projects like these, Carter has helped change the lives of so many, and now he's ready to provide you with solutions to even the most difficult tasks.

It is so important to feel at home in your own home. With Carter's Million Dollar Perspective and his thoughtful tips through-out this book, readers will have the tools to transform their home into their own space. You know you'll find me in the kitchen!

—*Rachael Ray*

INTRODUCTION

I was just eleven years old when my dad sat me down next to the family Ford, facing the left front tire. He said, "We need to replace the brake pads." By "we," we both knew he meant me. He made it clear that he was trusting me to do this, laid out all the tools I would need, and gave me a quick, easy-to-understand summary of how brakes work and how to replace brake pads. Did I mention I was eleven?

At first I was as excited as any kid would be. Every boy wants the chance to prove himself, to be like his dad. Then it hit me just how important a brake job really is. Cars can run well or they can run badly, but no matter how they run, they absolutely have to be able to stop.

I got nervous that I would screw up. No matter what my dad had said, brakes still seemed pretty complicated. It didn't even matter that he was going to inspect everything after I was done, or that he wasn't going to punish me no matter how it came out. Even though I knew all that, I felt entirely overwhelmed.

"I don't think I can do it," I told him, sitting there with a screwdriver in my hand.

"I bet if I gave you a million dollars to do it, you'd find a way."

Everybody has their "aha" moment. That was mine. A light clicked on. Put it that way, and a brake job starts to look pretty easy. So I went to work. I was careful and I concentrated on everything I did. I put everything I had into that brake job. Do it right, after all, and I would walk away with a million dollars. So I figured out how to take everything apart, how to put on the new brake pads, and how to reassemble everything just the way it was before I started. I finished up and went and found my father. He looked over everything, making these little noises in the back of his throat that meant he was really thinking about things. Finally, he gave me a big smile and a thumbs-up.

I can do a rock-solid brake job to this day, but the most valuable thing I took away from that experience is what I call "The Million Dollar Perspective." All of us face big challenges at one time or another. The way around those challenges is to trust yourself, use all the information you can lay your hands on, and never let yourself get defeated—you always have to remember that there's an answer somewhere. The idea that I can look at *everything* with the Million Dollar Perspective has helped me throughout my life. I used it in college, to get good grades in subjects that were hard for me. I used it to master carpentry. And I used it to rock my first home-design project.

Home design, decorating, and remodeling can be tricky. There are many ways to go about improving your interior space, but only one will lead to just the look you're after and a room that says exactly what you want it to say about your style. This much is true: You are totally capable of designing the home of your dreams.

Stunning marble tiles, sharp-looking cabinets, plenty of accessible work surfaces, and energy-efficient appliances positioned perfectly for efficient workflow . . . you can design a kitchen this terrific using Carter's Way and the Million Dollar Perspective.

Natural materials, such as the real wood, leather tables, the sisal rug, and natural fiber upholstery shown here, form the core of an environmentally friendly—and really stylish—room.

You don't need a design degree, an open-ended budget, or your own professional. You just need a basic philosophy and the proper inspiration for approaching the challenge, backed up by a rock-solid method you can easily follow. My philosophy and inspiration come from the Million Dollar Perspective. My method is what I call "Carter's Way." It's a process that has worked for me in dozens of different rooms and homes. Now I want it to work for you.

I'm writing this book because of all the people who come up to me at events, or write me, saying things like, "I wish I could make my kitchen look like the one on your last show," or, "If only I could have you work on my living room!" You don't need me in person. You don't need anybody else. You need my perspective and my method.

The book you hold in your hands isn't like any other home-design book. It's not about showing you all the cool rooms I've worked on in my career. It's not about listing every possible decorating and design option. You can find more options than you

can count at any big home center, paint outlet, hardware store, or furniture showroom. That's not this book. This book is all about empowering you and giving you a method that will be the ultimate design tool, like a Swiss army knife for home decorating and remodeling.

My goal with this book is to see the Million Dollar Perspective empower homeowners everywhere to jump fearlessly into their own home designs. I want them to have homes that express their personalities and are wonderful places to live. That perspective is half the battle; the other half is my way of doing it. I've tried to make it a simple, straightforward, adaptable process anybody can use. You'll find an in-depth explanation in chapter 1.

From there, each chapter covers a different area of the home. Some chapters cover more than one room, such as the dining room and kitchen, because the designs of those rooms are interconnected and best discussed in one place. Every chapter, though, puts Carter's Way to work in the real world, in real rooms. I think this is the best way to give you a sense of how to apply the process. That's why I've also included a Case Study in each chapter, featuring a project from one of my TV shows. These will allow you to follow along as I dissect how my team and I made the design decisions we made, worked to suit the preferences of the homeowner, and ultimately created a beautiful, livable space.

Along the way I've thrown in some boxes to provide a little more specific guidance. Anytime you come across "Carter's Law," you'll be reading a hard-and-fast rule I've learned through experience. I've also added a box I call "Deep Green Choices," because environmental concerns are important to me, and home decorating is an aspect of our lives where we can have a real, positive impact on the environment (not to mention the health of anybody who lives in the home) with little effort, expense, or sacrifice. Last, I've added boxes titled "You Can . . ." to give you guidance and inspiration to tackle easy changes and projects totally achievable by anyone with even modest do-it-yourself skills.

All that adds up to a lot of information. My hope is that you simply take what matters to you and put it to good use in your own home. I know from experience that with the right perspective and just a little bit of guidance, you can design spaces in your home that show off your style, make you happy, and make living there more fun, more fulfilling, and more healthy. Seems to me that any room design that does all that is well worth a million dollars!

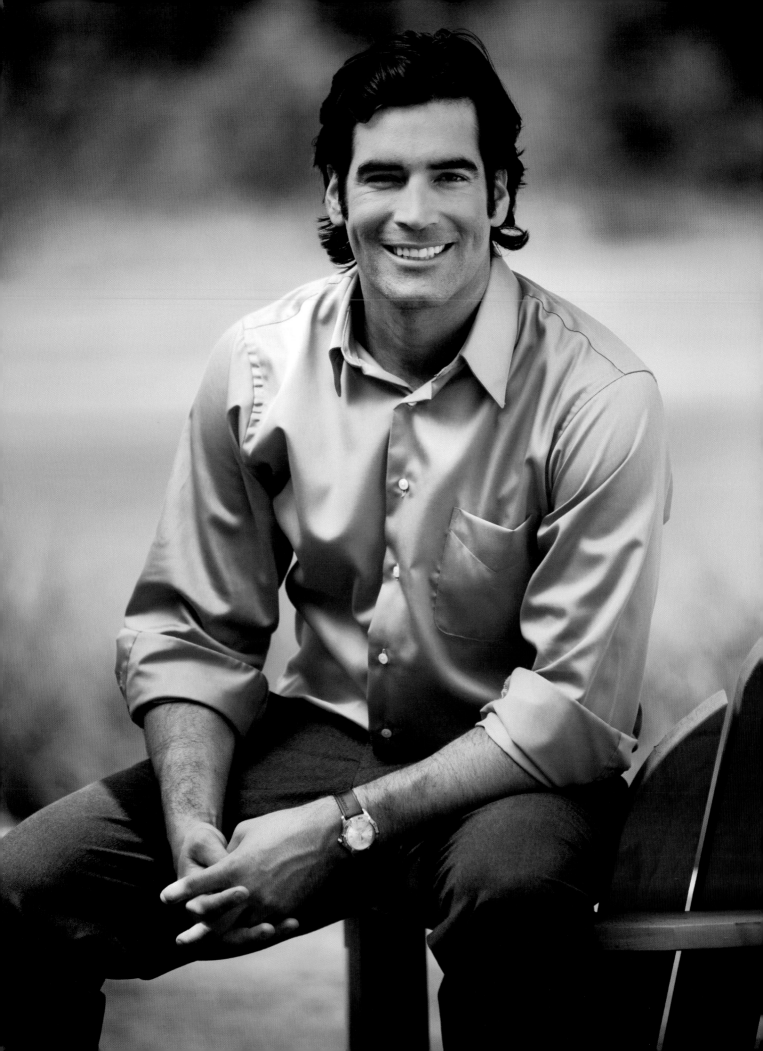

Chapter 1
CARTER'S WAY EXPLAINED

I once had someone ask me about my show *Carter Can,* "How do you do it? You go into a room and suddenly you pull it all together, and it looks great. It's like magic." It's not magic. It's a simple process born of design basics and lessons learned from experience. Instead of magic, I use Carter's Way.

Don't be afraid to flash your style, as long as it makes design sense. This room uses a black-and-white background to showcase two beautiful purple chairs. The placement of the furniture visually balances the room design. The sleek style, elegant window treatments, and faux zebra rug create a look that can only be described as glam and unique.

I'm not a formally trained designer. That's why, when I started working on my own TV show, I knew I needed a simple, adaptable design process that would work for all the different rooms we tackle over the course of a filming season. Not only is one home different from the next, everybody wants something different out of their living spaces. However, as much as every room is unique, there are in fact certain basic principles guiding any successful design. I developed Carter's Way around those universal guidelines. For ease of use, I break down the process into three interrelated parts: customized style, commonsense practicality, and realistic environmentalism. I look at these as legs on a triangle. Each one touches the other two, and there is no triangle without all three combined in the correct way.

They aren't step-by-step. Every point in developing a design—every decision you make—involves each of these in some way. Take buying a new couch for instance. The practical issue of cost will narrow the style options you can consider. You'll want a couch with a look that fits your customized style, works with your existing furniture, and that appeals to your own tastes. If you're a smart shopper, you'll put your environmentalist cap on when you check if the upholstery produces any volatile organic compounds that would compromise the air quality in your home. See how all three play a part in one simple choice?

All that said, let's start by looking closely at the idea of "customized style."

Customized Style

Style is the subjective part of the design process. Your personal tastes will differ from mine, which will be different from another person's. That's why I call this component "customized" style. You'll create your own unique look that has a strong foundation in the timeless principles that guide sound design. Just like every home—no matter what architectural style it is—has to have a foundation, every interior design stands or falls on a few universal principles. As long as these are in line, you can put your own stamp on your home design.

COLOR
You've probably been exposed to the basic principles of color many times, but just in case you haven't, here's a refresher. Individual colors can be divided between warm (reds and yellows) and cool (blues and greens). They can also be divided into receding and

Color basics are key to my method. A bathroom is usually best served by muted colors, whites, and neutrals. That's especially true of a bathroom like this with impressive features, such as a separate shower enclosure, luxury fixtures, and a picture window. The spa-like atmosphere, not the color scheme, takes center stage in this room.

advancing colors. Dark or warm colors advance—they look like they are closer to you. Cool or light colors recede, or appear to be farther away. (Useful effects to know about when you want to visually change a room's shape or perspective!)

Interior design involves grouping colors into "schemes" that can be complementary (those that sit across from each other on the color wheel), analogous (those that sit next to each other), or monochromatic (different shades and tints of the same color). There are more complicated color schemes, but these three are

CARTER'S LAW:
Test Drive All Your Colors

Colors need to be seen in the room in which they'll be used. Homeowners I meet seem to know this about paint, but they don't realize it's true about all the colored materials you'll incorporate into your design. You should sample new flooring material, countertop tiles, wall surface materials such as fabric wall coverings, and any other colored material you're thinking of using in the room. Designers often use what's called a sample board to gather all this material in one at-a-glance reference. They paint a big piece of plywood bright white and attach samples of all the materials. If this seems like too much work, you can just bring the materials into the room and display them near each other in a well-lit corner. View your samples the same way they'll be used—on flat surfaces for a countertop, and held up vertically for wallpaper.

the root of all of them, and you can play off them in your own design. Neutrals—brown, taupe, beiges, and off-whites—work with any other colors, as do black and white (technically called "achromatic"). A *shade* is a base color with black added to it, while a *tint* is a base color with white added to it (a *tone* is the color plus gray). All the particulars aside, you judge color by the way it looks in the actual space—there's no other way to do it. Whether you're looking for new wall paint, wallpaper, sofa fabric, or tile, manufacturers have made the process easy by collecting and organizing samples by color and combinations.

LIGHTING

Even though every room has its own lighting needs, there are three basic types of interior lighting used in any room. *Ambient* lighting is the term pros use for general light. It's the overall light that

A kitchen calls for versatile lighting, and this sleek, monochromatic room includes unique hanging fixtures, in-cabinet halogens, adjustable recessed ceiling fixtures, and a wall sconce. The lighting can accommodate virtually any situation.

spreads throughout the space and fills in shadowy areas, making the room safer to navigate and more inviting. Ambient fixtures include ceiling-mounted units and floor and table lamps. *Task* lighting is any light used to aid in a specific function. Undercabinet lights in the kitchen and a desk light in a home office are examples of task lighting. *Accent* lighting rounds out a room's lighting scheme, emphasizing decorative features or drawing attention itself. Frame-mounted art lights and cove lighting are examples of accent lighting.

Properly lit rooms usually include all three types of illumination to play up the strengths of the room's design and make the space easier to use. Lighting fixtures not only supply the illumination you need, they are also decorative elements. We'll talk more about lighting and fixtures particular to individual rooms in the chapters that follow. For now, understand that no single light source provides all the necessary lighting for a room; you'll need a combination if you want your design to look its absolute best.

LAYOUT

The layout of the room—where and how furnishings and other elements are positioned—determines how livable the room is, and how pleasing the interior design will be to the eye. Good layout is part art and part science, and it's a huge and critical part of any room design as far as I'm concerned. The space needed for proper navigation through a room is the science, and I've included guidelines throughout the chapters that follow. The more difficult part of layout is *composition,* which is all about proportion, scale, and balance. Furnishings need to balance one another, and be in balance with the dimensions and appearance of the room. Maybe you've seen a small bedroom stuffed to the gills with a "bedroom suite" of furniture bought as a complete set. That's an example of design imbalance, and a case where removing furniture might improve the room's layout immeasurably. Another example is a roll-arm overstuffed couch that a homeowner has paired with a dainty glass-topped coffee table. Everything you place in a room has some visual weight. You need to make sure that no one side of the layout or one area of the room carries a lot more visual weight than any other.

Because getting the relationship between furniture just right can be a bit of a challenge, I always recommend experimenting. As long as you're willing to move furniture in and out a room and play with different configurations, you'll eventually find your way to a balanced, attractive arrangement. I'll discuss examples of good layout practices in the chapters that follow.

The design theme you choose may drive everything from color choice to new furniture purchases. The homeowner who created this living room obviously went with sophisticated, understated elegance as the theme. Striped silk drapes and a tufted velvet coffee table reinforce the theme and create a luxurious look.

THEME

You can choose a standard theme such as "modern" or "country" that defines exactly how the room will look. More often than not, though, I find homeowners have their own ideas about theme and style. You'll probably want to define it in your own way, which is fine. Just be sure you are clear on what your "theme" means in terms of actual decorative elements. Dark and dramatic? Light and airy? Bright, witty, and full of energy? Are you the type that collects antiques, or are you more of an IKEA person? Do you like lots of comfy furniture and bric-a-brac filling up your space, or do you like an emptier nest, a place with a few well-chosen pieces and very little extraneous decoration? Define your theme to guide the decisions you'll make in your remodeling or design project.

The best way to develop room-specific ideas that embody your theme, tastes, and style is to keep a "style file." Collect sources of inspiration. I do. All the time. Sometimes I see a room in a magazine—not necessarily a design magazine. It could be a really cool ad, shot in a nice room. Sometimes it's just the cabinets or bed that strikes me as really handsome. Other times, I like the way a room is lit, or the appliances grab my attention. Room designs are put together in pieces, and collecting ideas that catch your eye for which pieces might go where is a great way of defining the particulars of your theme and style.

Beyond these basics, there are many techniques for establishing personal style in a room design. These include how you arrange wall-mounted art, what kind of storage you incorporate to prevent clutter, and the types of decorative accents you choose. Style indicators vary room to room, so that's how I cover them in this book.

Practically Speaking

The issue of customized style goes hand in hand with the second element in my process: commonsense practicality. It's easy to get carried away when you start looking at all the beautiful things you could include in a room design. The world is full of beautiful and impressive home furnishings. Catalogs are stuffed with fun and unique accents. Whole new floors, ceilings, and wall surfaces are waiting for you down the aisle of any large home center. Practicality brings you back down to earth. The most important and most practical piece of any design project is the budget. I've seen homeowners run out of money halfway through a room design; that makes no sense and it's the opposite of pretty. And frankly, I have been in some incredibly expensive homes, with million-dollar rooms, and some of them were the ugliest spaces I've ever seen. Just because you have money doesn't mean you have style.

BUDGET

You should start any design or remodeling project by deciding how much you can and are willing to spend on the design. Make this your line in the sand and don't go over it. A little discipline is necessary if you're going to have a stylish room that suits your home *and* your pocketbook. Keep track of costs as you go along. Budget is sure to narrow your choices, but it will also help you prioritize the elements of the design (do you want that great hand-painted tile backsplash *or* the new kitchen table?). You know what else? I find that budget (we're always on a pretty tight one on each of my shows) can light a fire under your creativity. Many times, I'll find ways to make something I've envisioned for a room, when the budget just can't

This isn't your mother's laminate countertop. It may look like actual granite, but this is the modern version of Formica, a much less expensive, still durable, and quite beautiful alternative to genuine stone countertops.

accommodate a brand-new purchase. I'm an experienced carpenter, so it's a little easier for me, but most people have it in them to construct small projects. I've also found that when a certain high-end material is too pricey for the project at hand, a little investigation often turns up an alternative with a similar appearance and much lower cost. I do this on my shows all the time.

Manufacturers know budget is an issue. That's why you can buy polyurethane wall moldings in place of pricier wood or plaster

CARTER'S LAW:
Measure for Access

Budget is the biggest practical consideration, but far from the only one. For instance, if you're looking to buy a new sofa, always take doorway and floor-space measurements to ensure you can get that piece of furniture into the room. This is a good rule of thumb for any new furnishing or appliance you're bringing in—from a dining room hutch to a refrigerator. Don't just measure one way; you need to know how high the ceilings are if you're looking at a poster bed. Consider the space carefully to take all practical issues into account.

versions, and why inexpensive laminate floors look convincingly like wood, stone, and other materials. I know budget is not exactly a fun part of the process, but it is essential. You'll thank yourself later when your room comes together beautifully without breaking the bank.

NATURAL LIGHT

Sunlight exposure is a major practical consideration. Television and computer screens set up opposite a bright, sunlit window are bound to feature glare spots, while furniture placed in a bright sunny spot should be dressed in fade-resistant upholstery. On the other hand, indoor plants positioned in a full-shade corner may quickly die. Wood, fabric, or laminate materials should never be placed too near a heat source such as a radiator, because the finish can fade and the surface will degrade over time.

YOUR ROOM OVER TIME

How the space will be used is a big part of practicality. It might require getting out your crystal ball and looking into the future a bit. It may be difficult to envision your newborn as a toddler, and then a rambunctious adolescent with friends and pets. It's worth thinking through, though, because that progression should play a role in the upholstery and surface treatments you choose, and any furniture you buy. I'll help you think through all these practical considerations in discussing specific areas in the house, but you should always keep practicality in mind when designing and remodeling.

The way I see it, twin bedside lamps are both a style element and practical necessity. These fixtures cast just enough light for the person on either side of the bed to read by, and the fixtures accent a room design that includes sumptuous bed linens and a striking hardwood floor.

Carter's Case Study:
Carter's Way in Practice in the Medford Kitchen

Taking on John and Shanee Medford's combination dining-room-and-kitchen project was a textbook study in how Carter's Way works. It was the couple's first house, and John had taken it upon himself to remodel the kitchen and dining room space. He got through the easy part of gutting the rooms. He discovered that there's not much precision or skill required to tear things apart, but unfortunately, that's not the case when you have to put them back together. John had jumped into the deep end of the pool and he needed someone to help him out.

The couple bought the home in large part because they liked the Spanish Mission–style architecture. They knew they wanted that style to come through in the new space,

The Medford kitchen stripped down to studs and plumbing. Now the hard part begins!

and they wanted the space to be functional and visually warm and appealing, with distinctive accents. They were also on board with including eco-friendly materials. We just had to make sure to stay on budget because there wasn't enough money for big-ticket luxuries. So, out of the gate, they were prime candidates for Carter's Way: They knew and could describe what customized style they wanted; they were realistic about practical concerns given the small space and tight budget; and they were very open to eco-friendly solutions.

We jumped right in, completing the "box" of the space. Designer Jinnie Choi chose a warm gold-yellow for the walls that would complement the variety of wood tones we were hoping to include. We picked a great solution for the floors—walnut engi-

This dining room alcove caught my eye right off; I knew it would make a perfect decorative feature.

neered flooring, in planks for the dining room, and thinner strips for the kitchen. This is a great solution any homeowner can use for two different functional areas in an open floor plan. By using the same surface material, visual continuity is maintained; but by using different widths of board run in different directions, we made it clear that the two parts of this open floor plan were distinctly different areas.

Carpenter Jake Scott worked with John to lay the floor. This type of "engineered" flooring comes in tongue-in-groove planks that the installer lightly taps into place. The floor took only a few hours to install and was a green option. The surface wood veneer uses much less wood than solid hardwood flooring, and engineered wood floors are durable and almost watertight. They are also less expensive than traditional hardwood because they can only be sanded and refinished twice before they need to be replaced. That still translates to decades of service.

The door opened into a bare space when we first stepped through it!

Next up, Shanee helped me put in the bottom cabinets for the kitchen. We went with bamboo because it's great for the environment; bamboo is a fast-growing grass that is considered a totally sustainable building material. Not to mention, it delivers a gorgeous look for a reasonable price.

Installing cabinets can be a lot easier than people think. It's a matter of taking the time to ensure the cabinets are level and plumb. The trick is to use shims as necessary beneath and behind the cabinet, where they will be out of sight and out of mind when you're done.

Before we were even halfway through the project, we'd already saved a bunch of money, created practical necessary storage, and done the environment a good turn in our choice of materials. And we were just getting started.

The dining room had new sheetrock, but not much else.

Jinnie Choi added a big splash of style in keeping with the Medfords' stated theme and design goals by painting port-wine colored rectangles on the wall, and then mounting flea-market-find wrought iron grill panels over the rectangles. The look was fantastic and you could see the Spanish Mission style beginning to appear. Touches like this go a long way toward reinforcing the customized style you've selected.

We left the passageway open between the two rooms, with rod-mounted curtains that could be used to partition off the dining room for special meals.

The Spanish Mission style is evident throughout this space, in the furnishings, colors, and wall art.

While Jinnie Choi was working on those accents, I was putting together the centerpiece of the dining room: a dining room table made completely from reclaimed lumber. I used reclaimed pine 2 x 6s for the top, planing them smooth. (If you want to use reclaimed lumber in a project but don't have a lot of woodworking tools, you can always have a local lumberyard or home center cut down, surface, or otherwise prepare the wood for a nominal fee.)

I built a frame from reclaimed pine 2 x 4s, using 6 x 6 posts for the legs. To give the table the feeling of an old world piece, I distressed the top by beating it with a stick with nails in it, and taking a blow torch to areas of the tabletop. I added iron bands across each end of the table in routed channels. Once we stained the table dark, it looked like it had been around for a hundred years.

The dining room was almost finished, but we needed countertops and backsplashes for the kitchen. Once again, we turned to eco-friendly and inexpensive options. We clad the plywood subsurfaces of the counters with granite overlays. Manufactured to the existing dimensions, these countertops reuse pieces and castoffs from the process of creating solid granite surfaces. Those odds and ends used to go straight to the landfill, but are now used to make shells that are installed right over a plywood base. The finished look is indistinguishable from a solid granite surface, goes in much quicker, and is coated with a food-safe resin that means the surface will never need to be sealed against stains. All for a lower cost than solid granite countertops would run!

We chose stone mosaic backsplashes made from stone veneer laminated to plywood to form complete panels. The panels were cut down to fit in the space between the countertops and the upper cabinets and were installed in a couple of hours.

Working with Jinnie, I made the most of the alcove in the dining room wall that had caught my eye. The alcove served no functional purpose, but we gave it a big decorative charge by painting the inside the same port-wine color Jinnie had used behind the iron grills. I nailed up three copper panels, which you can buy from any supplier of tin ceiling reproduction panels. A shelf with candles completed the look, and Jinnie added two matching floating shelves in dark wood along the wall in the dining room.

After installing the appliances, bringing in a sideboard and seating that matched the style of the dining room table, and putting up lighting fixtures that included a pillar candle chandelier, the two spaces couldn't have looked closer to the original design vision.

The Medfords were thrilled when they saw the finished rooms. Their customized style had come to life in a beautiful way, well within the practical limits of budget and function, with plenty of eco-friendly materials thrown in. A perfect example of what can be achieved using Carter's Way!

Painting the alcove red and lining it with candle shelves was a way to take an awkward architectural feature and turn it into a decorative bonus.

Granite overlay countertops bring a great sense of style to the modest sink area.

Although the space is small, the arrangement of cabinets and the location of stove and refrigerator are all about efficiency and ease of use—practicality in action.

At Home in the World

Realistic environmentalism is the third pillar of my design method. This issue matters deeply to me because it matters deeply to the world. I feel that whether you're designing your own home or someone else's, you have the moral responsibility to at least consider those eco-friendly choices that will affect the health and well-being of the people who live there.

However, when it comes to eco-friendly design, decorating, and remodeling, I don't take an all-or-nothing approach. I think far too often the message has been "you are either environmentally responsible or you're not." That's wrong. Living green means not being black and white. Being even a little bit green is better than not being green at all. I also try to open homeowners' eyes to the fact that environmental options have come a long way, and you

Slate? Ebonized wood? Engineered stone or laminate? Hardly. This is one of the greenest countertops going: a solid-surface material made of 100 percent post-consumer recycled paper and eco-friendly resins. Aside from being durable and available in a number of different lustrous colors and finishes, it's easy to work with and ages with a fine, warm patina. Going green often means going beautiful.

may be surprised at how simple, inexpensive, and stylish today's eco-friendly home design alternatives are. Sometimes, it's just a matter of wise shopping.

The fact is, many green home-design materials and fixtures are quite beautiful and competitively priced. Recycled glass counter-tops, reclaimed wood floors, linoleum, and extreme low-flow toilets are all available in a range of attractive designs at reasonable prices. In some cases, the environmentally responsible choice will be the only one you can make. Legislation phasing out incandescent bulbs and regulating water flow in bathroom fixtures means that you'll have to use fluorescent, halogen, or LED lighting in your room design and will determine the showerhead styles available. On the upside, a lot of these options translate to cost savings in the long run—on your energy and water bills, for example.

I'll also discuss some green design techniques for keeping rooms warm and well-lit to save energy. It's not hard to go green once you begin to understand your options, and I'm certainly not about to start demanding that people install photovoltaic panels on their roofs and buy composting toilets. Green design can be done in degrees, and you probably won't feel like you're giving up anything when you try it my way.

I hope I've made clear how inter-twined the three elements of my process are. The practical cost of a project depends on what elements of style and what eco-friendly features you choose and will limit or alter choices to a certain degree. Still, there are so many options on the market right now—in paint colors, surface finishes, lighting fixtures, and furniture—that exercising practicality and eco-friendly design practices is not going to hamstring you.

That's my way of remodeling, designing, and decorating interior spaces. I'm betting my million dollars that you'll find the method as useful as I have, as soon as you put it into practice in your next design project. Now it's time to see how Carter's Way works room by room.

Chapter 2
A FLAIR FOR COOKING, EATING, AND SOCIALIZING

Growing up, we had an eat-in kitchen. It was a place to gather and wolf down Nanu's (Grandma's) cooking, wash the dishes, and get on to whatever came next. The dining room was reserved for special occasions like holiday meals. Any other time, it was off-limits.

The modern kitchen isn't just a sterile factory for food prep. This room proves the point, with clerestory windows providing natural lighting, an island with built-in cabinets picking up the slack for the lack of wall cabinets, and a countertop table extension providing a cozy eat-in surface for drinks or dining. A photo mural creates a wonderful accent wall that introduces shades of the forested view from the windows. Overall, it's a calm, cool, and sophisticated multipurpose room design.

How times have changed.

Today's kitchen is pretty much the hub of the house. At any given moment, you might find Junior doing homework, Dad working on his computer, or Mom and a couple friends having a glass of wine while the lasagna cooks. Dinners have become family affairs, where everyone chips in with food prep. Meals are just as often savored as wolfed down.

The dining room has changed, too. These days, it's a more relaxed and adaptable space. It's still the gathering place of choice for special formal dinners and holidays, but it's also fair game for cocktail parties, informal get-togethers revolving around good food and drink, and even family game night. Redesigning or redecorating today's kitchen or dining room means taking all these uses into account. Because so much energy is used in the kitchen—and so much waste created—it's perhaps the best room in the house for having an impact with green design and sustainable practices.

Position dining room furniture for maximum ease of navigation and to create a visually logical look to the room. This dining room design establishes harmony through symmetry, placing the elegant table to run between two identical windows, with twin light fixtures featuring stylish drum shades.

Sketch Your Space

Start your kitchen and/or dining room redesign the same way I do—with a piece of paper and sharp pencil. Sketch a rough floor plan to scale and use it to help make design decisions. Sketching

Kitchens are first and foremost work spaces. A professional-quality range, an extra utility sink on the island, and a pot filler faucet all make this an efficient room even if more than one cook is working at the same time. A mix of shelves and glass-fronted cabinets and the combination of wood and marble work surfaces make the room incredibly stylish as well.

the dining room floor plan will be easy, but the kitchen sketch will take a little more attention to detail. Kitchens are busy work spaces that often have features such as islands complicating the layout. In either case, draw the room's basic dimensions, marking the location of windows, electrical outlets, and fixtures such as lights or built-in shelves. Add exact measurements for islands and other built-in features in the kitchen, and include arcs showing door swing for appliances such as refrigerators and stoves.

Trust me, a good sketch is your best friend in working out design specifics, and it can reveal surprising things about the space. A fresh dining room look can involve new ceiling, wall, and floor treatments, and decisions about furniture—whether you'll

CARTER'S LAW:
Allow Appropriate Space

We've all been in dining rooms or kitchens where the table is just too large for people to easily move around. Uncomfortable, right? You try to sit down and the back of your chair hits the wall, or the host tries to serve someone from a hot plate that can't be passed, and she can't reach the person. That's bad planning in action. Use the guidelines below to prevent cramped quarters.

- Kitchen work aisles should be at least 42 inches wide—48 inches if more than one person works in the kitchen at the same time.

- Kitchen designers suggest including at least two different work-surface heights. One should be between 28 and 36 inches above the floor, and another should be between 36 and 45 inches above the floor. This is to accommodate people of different heights. It's a great ideal, but if it's not possible, I don't lose any sleep over it.

- I like to see at least 2 feet of uninterrupted prep counter space on either side of the sink—the longer the better (36 inches is really ideal). Like all the counters in the kitchen, this space should be at least 16 inches deep, but 18 inches or more is best.

- Leave between 24 and 36 inches of space out from the edge of a table for diners to sit and move in and out of chairs comfortably. If people need to walk behind seated diners, allow between 36 and 48 inches.

- Islands or countertop eating areas should allow a space at least 20 inches deep underneath for a seated person's legs, and 24 inches of countertop width for each place setting.

repurpose what you have or buy new. Getting that all right means paying attention to entrance and exit pathways (often one and the same), and allowing the space you'll need to move comfortably around the table. Develop the ideal setup by playing with the position of cutouts representing furniture on your floor plan sketch.

A kitchen redesign is a little more complicated. Use your sketch to experiment with the relationships between seating, work spaces, and storage, and to come up with a formula that works for you, your family, and guests. No matter what, always start with the sacred "work triangle." The function of any kitchen centers on this triangle, formed by the location of the refrigerator, stove, and the prep/sink area. Research has shown that to create the most efficient kitchen, the legs of the triangle must add up to at least 12 feet, but no more than 26 feet. No leg of the triangle

Sharp white cabinets provide the background to a very efficient kitchen design. Sleek, easy-to-clean granite counters and abundant rail hanging storage make food prep and cooking a snap in this space.

should be smaller than 3 feet or be blocked by a structure such as an island or table. Depending on how extensive your redesign will be, you may want to play around with the location of the cooktop, countertops, or refrigerator while you're sketching, using the opportunity to create a space in which it's easier to work.

Your kitchen design should honestly reflect how you use the space. Are you a gourmet home chef who escapes the pressures of the day by cooking spectacular four-course dinners? If so, focus on work areas first, with high-grade appliances and easy-to-access cookware storage. On the other hand, maybe you're a busy soccer mom with three growing kids to feed, and friends popping over on a regular basis. In that case, prepared-food storage will be more important in your kitchen, and comfort will be the hallmark of the room's design.

Carter's Case Study:
The Ringler Kitchen

I first met Michelle Ringler after two contractors left her high and dry in the middle of a kitchen renovation. Michelle was understandably at wits' end after six months of not having a usable kitchen, and I brought my *Carter Can* team in to give her some help. She wanted a space where she could relax over breakfast, indulge her love of cooking, and entertain friends.

Every design starts with some kind of style indicator. It can be a swatch of paint, a restored antique stove, or just an idea. In Michelle's case, it was the new cabinets and island that were the only pieces of her kitchen puzzle that had been installed and finished. The dark ebony stain, along with her stainless steel appliances, established a sophisticated and modern design theme.

Her kitchen had a functional rectangular floor plan, with the island dominating the space between the work area and the eat-in space. The simple, contemporary cabinets featured frosted-glass fronts, adding elegance to the room. As Michelle described it, "Contemporary, sophisticated, and yet still warm."

There was a lot left to do. We needed to decide on a wall color, choose countertops, and pick a flooring to go over the exposed subfloor. Michelle wanted the materials used in the space to be eco-friendly. I was glad to hear it.

Given how much it impacts the design in a space, we started with the floor. Michelle fell in love with the cork strip flooring I suggested. The light brown speckled appearance worked perfectly with the black cabinets and island. More important, cork is a renewable material that is naturally antibacterial and waterproof—key benefits for a kitchen. We selected easy-to-install, floating tongue-in-groove strip flooring that required no adhesive or nailing. Michelle's boyfriend and I installed it in a few hours without breaking a sweat.

Next up were the countertops. We settled on a beautiful quartz composite in a light taupe to complement the black cabinets. Quartz composite is an engineered stone material that resists heat and damage from wear every bit as well as a natural stone like granite. It never needs to be sealed and, because it's engineered, the texture and pattern are attractively uniform. It's also a green material, requiring no quarrying or other depletion of natural resources.

I wanted to add additional storage, because you can never have too much storage in a kitchen. Michelle agreed to a wall-mounted glass-front cabinet and wall-mounted bar cabinets next to her breakfast nook. These features would make the area adaptable so that it could be used for both casual meals and upscale entertaining. Carpenter Jake Scott crafted the new glass-fronted storage cabinet with the same distinctive bent-wood detail that defined a beautiful armoire in the front hall. Tie different rooms together—and create design continuity throughout the house—by replicating signature elements like these room to room.

The walls needed color that could hold up to the large amount of black in the space. Designer Jinnie Choi suggested a muted eggplant. Although purples can overwhelm a space, choosing one with gray undertones got us to a tamer wall color that complemented the black, while providing a very sophisticated background hue. It was also light enough to offset what was becoming a dark space.

The island centers the design of the completed kitchen and serves as a place to enjoy breakfast or for friends to have a drink while Michelle cooks.

The kitchen really began to take shape with the floor, countertops, and walls all completed. We moved on to those accents that bring polish to any kitchen design. We chose recycled-glass subway tile for the backsplash. Michelle flipped over the sophisticated high-gloss beige appearance, and it fulfilled her eco-friendly requirement nicely, because it's made from waste material, requiring modest resources and energy in manufacturing. The tile itself is easily recycled when it comes time to replace it. Recycled glass tile comes in every shade of the rainbow, and finishes range from the high gloss you would expect to surprising matte textures.

You can install a tile backsplash yourself. It's a lot easier than tiling something like a bathroom floor, and manufacturers have made it even more so by grouping smaller tiles on mesh backing that maintains perfect spacing between tiles. Instead of installing each individual tile, Michelle worked with square-foot sections. Even with mixing the mortar (simply add water and mix with a drill attachment), Michelle and Jinnie were able to install the entire backsplash in less than two hours. An elegant gray grout provided the perfect finishing touch for the surface. Michelle had never done tile work before and was amazed at how easy it was and how beautiful the result turned out to be. I guarantee you can do it, too.

We finished up with the lighting. The right lighting is essential in a busy work space like a kitchen. In Michelle's case, we also needed to brighten up a room that featured a lot of black surfaces. We supplemented the ceiling's recessed lighting with two sleek pendants over the sink. Over-sink lighting is a must-have for any kitchen to be truly usable. We also added undercabinet lighting that can be turned on when food is being prepped on the counters and off when Michelle is entertaining.

I made some custom stools for the island, creating seating for guests. Although I designed the stools to suit Michelle's kitchen specifically, you can pick from an incredible variety of stools available at retail, in any design style you might use in your kitchen. We also added a tall cafe table and tall chairs to create a cozy breakfast nook that doubles as a relaxing area to share a glass of wine with a friend. It helps to look for versatile pieces when you choose your kitchen furniture.

Interior cabinet lights and undercabinet lighting fixtures ensure that the lighting in the kitchen is adjustable to any mood and that work surfaces are always well lit.

Cabinet-face decals that match the wall decorations are an inspired touch. Frosted-glass cabinet fronts add the same elegance that clear glass fronts do without the need to keep what's stored inside neat and tidy at all times.

A tall cafe table is a great space-saving option for a smaller eat-in kitchen.

YOU CAN . . . Decorate with Decals

Jinnie added some decorative punch with white vinyl wall decals. You can find lots of suppliers online, and the potential designs are nearly unlimited. Suppliers offer words, numbers, and an amazing variety of graphics like the flower stems we used (opposite page). You can even order your own design as a custom decal. Whichever you end up choosing, they are reasonably priced. We spent less than $75 per decal (price depends on complexity) and once you have them in hand, you'll be amazed at how easy they are to work with. Even if you've never worked with a stencil or decal, you'll have no problem using these. Follow the supplier's instructions, but basically you simply stick the decal where you want it, smooth out any bubbles, and then peel off the protective top layer. It took less than an hour for Jinnie to apply two wall decals and place a smaller one on the inside of a glass cabinet front. If you ever get tired of the decals, they are simple to remove with a little patience and a utility knife equipped with a sharp blade.

Choose a Centerpiece for the Room

Once you've finalized your sketch of the space and thought through where all the components and appliances should go, you have a redesign blueprint. The actual design will be driven by a "centerpiece." Dining rooms are almost always centered on the dining room table and chairs. The centerpiece in a kitchen can be an idea (high-tech, stainless steel), a general theme or period (funky, retro, country), or even a hallmark feature (vintage stove, sleek cabinets, special tile). You'll refer back to that centerpiece to help you make decisions throughout the design process. Once you've settled on what your particular centerpiece will be, move forward in making the decisions about individual design elements that surround the centerpiece.

A centerpiece dining room table and chair set as chic as this one deserves to dominate the dining room. However, notice that enough room has been left around the table for easy and unimpeded movement, with a matching hutch well out of the way of traffic flow.

The Gourmet Background

I like to start with the walls and ceiling in a kitchen or dining room, because they are large surfaces that can set the tone in terms of color (and sometimes texture and pattern), contrasting or complementing the centerpiece. Most homeowners choose to paint the walls because there are so many color options and because painting is easy and quick. Not to mention, you can repaint a wall on a whim if you ever decide to switch up your palette.

Look overhead first. Ceilings are almost always painted flat white and left unadorned, but that doesn't have to be the case. I don't usually look to make a statement with the ceiling, but a dining room can be a great place to try out a different look. A tray ceiling adds drama to a room. It's one of those features that draws the eye and really pops out. Installing an actual tray ceiling (where the center rectangle of the ceiling is higher than the outer border) is quite an undertaking. If you're not ready to tear up your existing ceiling, you can get some of the decorative bang of a tray ceiling without actually constructing one. Use two different shades of beige to paint the illusion of different ceiling levels. Paint a thin border in the darker color to outline the rectangle, and then paint inside the rectangle with the lighter color. It fools the eye, which reads the lighter field of color as receding, creating the illusion of depth.

I find that walls are a much better place to get creative. Paint is certainly not your only wall-covering option. Wallpaper is great if you want a patterned surface, or if you have a period-style home

A mid-range green is a great choice for a kitchen. The wall color and bright white molding help to unify the two adjacent rooms, and the bright white ceiling in the kitchen provides some contrast to a fairly low-key and dark design.

Sometimes bold is simply beautiful. This kitchen features a stunning analogous color scheme dominated by intense blue cabinet panels. It may not be for everyone, but this look works in this kitchen, adding life and an upbeat feel, and actually makes the room seem bigger in the process.

and wallpaper more accurately represents the period. But if you paper your dining room, I'd suggest adding a chair rail, so that chairs bumping into the wall don't damage the paper (a chair rail also adds dimension to the room). Wallpaper designs give you the opportunity to change the perception of the room. Vertical stripes will make the ceiling seem higher, while horizontal stripes will visually stretch the room, making it seem more spacious. Big pattern elements tend to make a room look smaller, while small patterns make it look larger. But keep in mind that the more complex the wallpaper's design, the more difficult it will be to line up the pattern correctly at the seams.

You can also use a solid-color wall covering to add texture and avoid dealing with patterned designs. Seagrass creates a truly sophisticated monochromatic look. Leather, although very expensive, makes for a one-of-a-kind wall surface that isn't right for every room, but can be truly stunning when used in the appropriate dining room (think dark wood detailing and brass fixtures).

I'd suggest you be absolutely certain you love the look before wallpapering a kitchen. Heat and moisture are the enemies of wall coverings, and a busy kitchen spells abuse for wallpaper and

Kitchens call for unique wallpaper such as this block pattern in shades of orange. Not only is this paper stunning and the perfect complement to the light and dark cabinetry, it's also durable—it's paper-backed vinyl that is scrubbable and peelable.

similar surfaces. Where wallpaper is your choice, go with a sturdy, "scrubbable" vinyl-coated paper. These days, large, bold patterns are in vogue, although you should choose a pattern that makes sense with the cabinetry and other design elements in the room (also, bold patterns are generally used in large rooms—they'll overwhelm a small space). Wall murals—photographic or illustrated scenes on paper—are wonderful choices for an accent wall.

Wainscoting—wood panels and molding installed over the bottom half of a wall—is a traditional treatment for formal dining rooms. Installing wainscoting is a lot of work and can add a lot of cost to your redesign project (especially if you have a pro do it), but the look is undeniably attention-getting and distinctive. The wainscoting itself can be stained or painted, whichever best complements the upper half of the wall. You can buy complete wainscoting kits with polyurethane panels and molding, as a less expensive and easier alternative to real wood panels.

Go sleek and sophisticated in your kitchen by cladding walls in the same wood veneer used on the cabinet faces (the wood should be distinctive, as this brown-stained pine certainly is). The design of this room blends shelves with the wall surface, a treatment that would lend a clean modern look to the walls of any kitchen.

Painting the walls is the most popular option, but paint shouldn't equal boring. You can create a lot of visual interest with the right color combinations, especially when you use small splashes of contrasting or bold color throughout the room.

Special painting effects are another way to add excitement. For instance, sponged or rag-rolled walls provide an appropriately elegant mood and look of sophistication in the dining room. Even if the treatment is only used on a single accent wall, it's an eye-grabbing feature. Accent walls in bold colors can jazz up a kitchen or dining room. A lime-green partition wall adds zest to a bright white kitchen scheme. A deep chocolate brown end wall lends richness to a beige dining room, making the room more inviting.

Here's a great idea for a busy kitchen in a household full of kids and adults: Paint a large square or rectangle on a little-used wall using metallic paint. Then cover the metallic paint with chalkboard

YOU CAN . . . Choose Kitchen Colors That Work

Many people gravitate right to white or beige for their kitchens. But you can have dramatic color without it looking gaudy or overwhelming the space. Trust your instincts and start with colors you love. I'm a fan of blue, so I chose a bluish gray for my kitchen. Just about any sample can now be matched in paint, thanks to the magical computerized color-matching technology at most large paint stores and home centers. Many of these stores also offer pint-sized sample jars so you can test colors for little cost. Even if you have to buy a quart, the cost is still modest. Don't just buy the exact color, though. At the very least, test a darker and lighter version of the color, if not a totally different hue. Paint squares of the samples on a wall and live with them for a week or so, checking them under different lighting, day and night.

paint. Apply two coats and let them dry. Then cover the surface with chalk and erase it. This will ensure the longevity of the surface. Now you have a surface on which you can write messages or hang artwork or other paper using magnets. Use the space to write recipes, messages, or as a changeable family photo album.

Regardless of what paint you choose and how you use it, you'll want to select the right sheen. Dining room walls are usually covered in eggshell, or in flat if the walls in most of the other rooms are flat. Kitchens should be painted in an eggshell or—if the kitchen is a high-traffic area—satin finish. It should go without saying that you want to seek out low- or no-VOC (volatile organic

You can go dark and dramatic with the colors and textures in a kitchen, but it's always wise to provide a little balance. Here, the dark brick and ebony cabinets are contrasted with white counters and a white open-beam ceiling structure complete with skylights. The lighter elements, including a yellow wall, actually give the dark surfaces more visual power, while ensuring the space doesn't seem cavelike.

compounds) paint, especially for rooms where the focus is on cooking, eating, and drinking. Low- and no-VOC paints continue to improve and come down in price, year after year.

Kitchen and Dining Room Flooring Options

You might be happy with the floors in your kitchen and dining room, in which case you can jump right to choosing other surfaces, such as countertops and cabinets. But if replacing the floor is part of your redesign, you've got many, many options in front of you, especially in a kitchen. Once upon a time, kitchen floors were limited to linoleum, vinyl, or ceramic tile. Thankfully, that's not the case anymore. Today there are so many alternatives you won't have to look hard to find just the right floor for your kitchen, your budget, and the way you live.

This kitchen surface may look like stone, but the floor and backsplash are actually ceramic tile. Lower cost, same visual dynamite!

CERAMIC AND PORCELAIN TILES

These types of tiles are still hugely popular for kitchen floors. No wonder, because they're easy to clean, durable, and beautiful. You'll find tiles in just about any color you could want, and with wonderful hand-painted designs and patterns if you're willing to spend a little more (even custom designs for the right price). Ceramic and porcelain tiles also come in finishes from high-gloss to matte, and with prices that run from very modest to incredibly expensive. These materials are green, because the resources and processes used to make them are abundant, natural, and recyclable. The finished floor emits no toxic gases. On the downside, individual tiles are susceptible to breakage if you drop something heavy like a cast-iron pot, and the grout lines can collect dirt and food particles. Tile floors are also labor intensive to install, and require a fair amount of skill to get right.

LINOLEUM AND MARMOLEUM

These are some of the most environmentally friendly floors. Manufactured from all-natural and renewable ingredients including flax, sawdust, and other organic materials, linoleum—and its modern counterpart marmoleum—don't off-gas or produce any detrimental by-products. Both are also naturally antibacterial and antimicrobial, making them spectacular choices for a kitchen where kids, pets, and dropped food are likely to collide. Marmoleum comes in the same hard-to-install sheet flooring that linoleum does, but it's also offered as easy-to-install, click-together strips (it's slightly less durable than linoleum). In either form, the flooring has many faces, including solid colors or geometric designs in bold or subdued shades, convincing faux-wood and faux-stone surfaces, and more. What's more, the material is soft and warm underfoot and is a forgiving landing pad for dropped glassware. Marmoleum is so versatile that it's increasingly being used outside the kitchen and bath, including in dining rooms.

STONE TILES

Stone can bring an unmistakably opulent look and feel to a kitchen and, where appropriate, the dining room as well. The selection is mind-boggling. Choose the pure sophistication of sealed marble, the rough-hewn appeal of slate, or the unusual surface variations of limestone. You can go with sedate colors such as the beige or light brown of a sandstone or travertine, or dive into the deeper, more vibrant colors of granite or marble (pinks, purples, blacks!). Foot-square tiles are the norm, but you can opt for the more rustic appeal of stone mosaics. Ask before you buy, because depending on the stone you select, you may be faced with regular maintenance to reseal the surface. Although stone tiles are produced from abundant natural resources, manufacturing and transport introduce a significant amount of carbon into the environment. They are still considered green, however, because a stone tile floor can last the life of the home. That longevity should be considered when pricing stone tiles, because up front they are some of the priciest flooring—especially when you add in the cost of installation.

CORK

Cork is on par with linoleum as a truly green flooring choice. The material is renewable, harvested from long-living trees as a regular part of the trees' growing cycle. Cork flooring resists mold and mildew and is hypoallergenic. It's also amazingly soft and warm underfoot. Cork comes in many shades of brown (some manufacturers even tint the material to offer a broader spectrum of colors), with subtle but eye-catching surface patterns. Although it is more expensive than marmoleum and some other kitchen flooring, it is simple to install. The flooring comes as click-together strips that are laid in a floating floor. Most suppliers sell the flooring prefinished with a protective polyurethane topcoat, although some require you to apply an additional coat.

This modern dining room set may look like it's sitting on a wood floor, but it's actually high-quality laminate.

LAMINATE

Easy to install, laminate flooring has given the homeowner an inexpensive option that convincingly mimics just about any look, from wood to stone to ceramic tiles. The floor is constructed of a base layer of processed wood waste, over which are laid a photographic paper and a hard, protective melamine topcoat. Quality laminate floors are durable and look great. They can be installed in a day with very modest DIY skills and hardly any tools, because most come in click-together floating-floor styles.

VINYL

One of the most popular materials among home-owners, vinyl flooring is often used for kitchens and baths. Available in both sheet and adhesive tile formats, vinyl flooring is manufactured in a vast array of colors and surface effects. Relatively inexpensive, the surface texture can be completely flat, or molded into relief, copying the look of tile or stone surfaces. Vinyl is comfortable, cushiony, and warm underfoot. However, I tend to avoid vinyl for the simple reason that it is one of the most environmentally damaging materials in the home. The production of vinyl flooring creates a laundry list of toxic waste products, and the flooring itself is associated with significant off-gassing—linked by some studies to childhood asthma and other medical conditions.

YOUR FLOORING CHOICE

Every flooring has its pros and cons. Ultimately, those should be balanced against the look and feel that you're after. Choose flooring that makes the most sense for you in terms of comfort, ease of installation, durability, and expense. Select strip or sheet flooring carefully, with an eye to how well the look of the floor integrates into the overall design scheme of the kitchen. Bold patterns or colors in the floor can pull attention away from other showcase features, such as unique countertops or cabinetry. I consider the floor a backdrop for the other design elements in the room and tend to be a little conservative in my choice of flooring.

Tile floors give you the chance to introduce interesting textures and patterns without overwhelming the design. However, you still want to keep the tile from dominating. The size of the tiles themselves will also have an impact. Larger tiles tend to make a room seem larger and less busy. Smaller, standard 4-inch-square tiles have the opposite effect. A floor laid of larger tiles is also usually less expensive and somewhat easier to install.

If the dining room shares a single open space with the kitchen, it makes sense to continue a new kitchen floor into the dining area. Usually, though, ceramic or stone tiles—or any floor that looks like either of those—is probably not the best choice for the dining room. Whichever floor you choose for the dining room, it should complement the kitchen floor if the two visually flow into one another. If they are connected only through a doorway, you have more design latitude in choosing entirely different floors. Although wood floors or carpet are the most common choices for dining rooms, I'd suggest you consider a laminate faux-wood strip floor. The fact that you

A dining area rug serves as a stage for this dining room set. The Oriental rug is the ideal style for the Asian-inspired lines of the storage pieces, and it works great with the black chairs and farmhouse slab table. The rug helps define the room and adds to a look full of simple elegance.

can clean a laminate floor, and that dishes are less likely to break when dropped on one, makes this particular material well-suited for dining-room duty.

Appliance Appearance

Appliances have a pretty significant effect on the look of any kitchen design. If you're sticking with your existing appliances, make sure you keep them in mind when choosing kitchen colors and fixtures.

Narrow the options when choosing new kitchen appliances such as refrigerators, electric stoves, and dishwashers based on the space you have available for the appliance and the look that matches your design. Unless you're renovating the kitchen down to the bare bones, any new appliances will likely need to fit existing dimensions. That will limit the models and styles you can consider. Appliance finish trends vary over time, but the most timeless looks are stainless steel, white, and black. Stainless steel complements a wide range of kitchen styles but is hard to keep streak-free. White appliances work with many color schemes and they are easy to clean because it's easy to see the dirt (and the coated surface comes in textured as well as smooth). Black is the least adaptable appliance color, usually only appropriate for darker or more dramatic color schemes.

Stainless steel is the most common finish for kitchen appliances because it blends well in kitchens from modern to traditional. The look is handsome, especially in well-appointed kitchens like this one, featuring multiple ovens, glass chillers, a dishwasher, and a refrigerator.

DEEP GREEN CHOICES: Appliance Efficiency

Among the most important decisions you'll make in choosing new kitchen appliances is whether or not to buy Energy Star-rated models. In reality, there's little reason not to do so. Energy Star is a program established as a partnership between the U.S. Environmental Protection Agency and the U.S. Department of Energy. The goal was to conserve precious natural resources and help consumers save money, and the program has been wildly successful doing both. It sets stringent standards for manufacturers and models to meet to earn the rating. You'll know an Energy Star-rated appliance when you see one because it will be wearing the yellow Energy Star sticker and label.

Energy Star appliances are typically more expensive than those that don't qualify, but part of the mandate of the program is to ensure that the consumer realizes an energy cost savings that will return the difference in the original purchase price, in "a reasonable amount of time" (that usually means within three years, and sometimes within one). According to the Department of Energy, the program helped consumers save a total of almost $17 billion on utility bills in a single year, while preventing 30 million cars' worth of greenhouse gases from entering the environment. Replacing all your existing kitchen appliances with Energy Star models can save you a third or more on your utility bill. The Energy Star label lists the average savings per year you can expect with the unit. Also keep an eye out for appliances carrying a CEE tier I, II, or III rating. This means the appliance exceeds the requirements for Energy Star rating and points to exceptional energy efficiency. Last, I'm the spokesperson for the Council of Responsible Energy, and as such, I promote the use of natural gas–powered appliances. Natural gas is clean, abundant, and safe when used correctly in the home.

Work-Surface Chic

Kitchen design is often ruled by countertops and backsplashes. A kitchen with gnarly and chewed-up counters and bare back-splashes will never look good, no matter what you do to the cabinets, floors, or walls. You're in luck though, because there are a wealth of countertop options. It's not hard to find more than one that will suit the overall style you have in mind. Then it's just a matter of what your wallet has to say about it.

In addition to being a big style indicator in the kitchen, countertops are also high-use work surfaces. How much you cook—and how and what type of prep you regularly do—may play a part in your final choice. Backsplashes—that wall space between the top of the counter and the bottom of the wall-mounted cabinets—are more about pure looks. But the surface should also be cleanable. Let's take a look at the countertop materials first.

Gorgeous work surfaces, like the marble top on this island table, can set the tone for a whole kitchen. Here, the sleek counters fit right in with the stunning cabinetry, modern pendant lights, and high-end appliances.

STONE

Granite, sandstone, travertine marble, and other quarry products are all stunning as counters. However, they'll take a big bite out of your budget, and some require regular maintenance. Still, stone surfaces are the epitome of luxury. They're also cook-friendly surfaces, resistant to high temperatures and easy to clean. Stone is a fairly green choice once installed. A stone countertop will likely last

If you're enchanted with the look of marble and granite—but less so with the price—take a look at quartz. This quarry stone is just as beautiful as other stone countertops, but much harder and with a nonporous surface that doesn't need sealing.

YOU CAN . . . Go Counter Colorful

If most counter choices are too tame for you, or you just want to add a splash of seriously vibrant color to a new kitchen island or small counter area, consider Pyrolave. This incredibly durable material is quarried from volcanic stone, cut into slabs, and enameled to create a heat- and scratch-resistant, waterproof, and fade-proof colored surface. The surfaces are an unusual look and the bold colors may not be perfect for every kitchen, but they bring a real charge wherever the kitchen color scheme includes a sense of adventure.

the life of your home, and that longevity is reflected in a relatively high cost. Figure on amortizing the up-front hit over decades of use. Add in the cost of installation, because you're going to need a couple sure-handed professionals to move and install stone countertops correctly.

ENGINEERED STONE

This is a less pricey alternative to natural stone, but one that captures much of the beauty. Engineered stone countertops are manufactured by combining small fragments of the stone, such as marble or granite, with a polymer base. This creates a surface with a uniform look in the color—if not the pattern. Many of these types of countertops are susceptible to damage from heat (quartz composite is relatively heat-proof), although scratches and abrasions can be buffed out. The countertop doesn't off-gas or otherwise add toxins to the home. Engineered stone countertops are ordered and made to your dimensions, and are normally installed by pros.

This is just one of the many looks offered in engineered stone countertops. You'll find a wealth of surface appearances, suitable to just about any kitchen decor style.

SOLID-SURFACE

Solid-surface countertops continue to grow in popularity because they are priced on par with other high-end choices, and they come in many different looks, from solid color to convincing imitations of marble and granite. They can even be produced in custom-blended colors or patterns. The countertops are fabricated of proprietary synthetic formulas, which don't contain toxins or release harmful gases, and can be manufactured to just about any size or configuration, without seams. Solid-surface countertops are often molded with a sink, backsplashes, and other features as integral parts of the countertop—the most interesting feature of this option. It's practical as well as aesthetic: no lips, edges, or seams to trap dirt and water. Scratches are sanded out and most types of solid-surface counters are sealed against stains. Heat may damage the countertop. And, as a synthetic composition, the countertops don't biodegrade, putting a bit of a crimp in the "green" cred of this surface.

BUTCHER BLOCK

Woods are not the wildly popular options they once were, but they are still wonderful materials for use as kitchen work surfaces. A wide variety of hardwoods are used in countertops, so you can choose from many different appearances, from blonde to nearly black to striped. The range of prices runs from the modest to the obscenely expensive. The cost is affected by thickness, the wood species, and other factors such as inlays. Butcher block is a traditional food prep surface, even though it can collect bacteria if not kept clean. Hardwood countertops require care and caution because chopping, cutting, or setting super hot pots on the surface are all going to leave marks. They also have to be kept away from heat sources such as the vents on stoves and dishwashers and require special cleansers that won't degrade the finish.

Wood can be an environmentally responsible countertop choice, depending on what wood you choose and where it was harvested. The greenest are FSC-certified (Forest Stewardship Council), reclaimed wood, or sustainable varieties such as bamboo. Some manufacturers even offer versions crafted from recycled paper and wood waste products. Eco-friendly versions will be finished in low- or no-VOC stains, oils, or sealants.

LAMINATES

Formica and other laminates are perennial favorites for their low cost, incredible range of colors and patterns, and surprising durability. Laminate countertops are crafted from a thick layer of plastic glued onto a particleboard or plywood base. These countertops are available in every color imaginable, a dizzying array of patterns, and imitations of stone and other natural surfaces. Many manufacturers use recycled wood in the base and VOC-free adhesives, making the surfaces harmless in the home. Laminate countertops are fairly easy to install, but you should be well skilled in the use of a saw and router.

CERAMIC, GLASS, OR PORCELAIN TILES

Tiles are regularly used in countertops in traditional or contemporary kitchens. The finished surface is appealing and can be extremely

Laminates have come a long way, and you might be surprised at the amazing number of intriguing looks—such as this countertop that convincingly mimics soapstone without the maintenance.

unique to your kitchen. These tiles are also a very eco-friendly option, and you can play with the design by picking different size tiles for the countertop or mixing and matching colors or patterns to make your own design. Properly installed, tile countertops are waterproof, but they leave something to be desired as work surfaces because they are uneven for chopping, and the grout lines collect dirt and grime. Avid cooks usually choose another material for their kitchens.

STAINLESS STEEL AND CONCRETE

Though I wouldn't recommend them for everyone, you might also think about stainless steel or concrete countertops. Stainless steel screams professional cook, but the surface is cold to the touch, hard to keep streak-free, and really only a look that you'd want if your kitchen is high-tech and focused solely on cooking.

Concrete has shed its sidewalk roots and come into the kitchen in a big way. Concrete countertops can be polished and left in a natural color, for a modern "loft-style" look, or tinted in any of a number of hues. I have concrete surfaces in my house and I love the look. I don't seal the surface, letting the stains show instead of polishing the surfaces every year. I like the look of the stains because it gives the surface more character and works with the style of my home. Wet concrete can also be stamped with an imprint stencil for a unique texture. Many suppliers cast the concrete in place, although it's better to buy countertops precast to match your dimensions and installed once dry. Either way, this

Concrete counters offer a durable and interesting look, and in addition to the natural color shown here, they can be tinted in a range of colors, as well as white and black.

DEEP GREEN CHOICES: Kitchen Countertops

Some of the most alluring countertops made from recycled materials are those created of post-consumer paper products. As this example clearly shows, recycled paper countertops have the warmth and visual depth of wood, but come in solid colors and appearances that capture all the beauty of stone, leather, and other natural materials.

If you're open to spending a little bit more on your countertops, you can do the world and yourself a big favor by selecting from among a medley of extremely eco-friendly countertop options. Many of these offer distinctive appearances unlike any other type of countertop, while some mimic the look of traditional materials. Most are produced entirely or mostly from recycled materials, thereby taking those materials out of the waste stream and preserving whatever resources would have gone into making a new countertop.

Products like Shetkastone, which uses recycled paper products and binders to create solid-colored countertops, and EcoTop, a solid-surface mix of bamboo fiber, recycled wood, and a relatively inert binder, offer straightforward formed surfaces in a modest palette of colors. You can also find countertops made of recycled aluminum, as an alternative to stainless steel, and recycled concrete. Several manufacturers use recycled stone waste in products such as Lithistone, which uses a natural binder to hold together sand, pieces of stone, and other recycled materials, in a countertop that looks much like a solid-surface product. Some of these can even be custom tinted or manipulated to create one-of-a-kind looks. Among the most arresting are those made of recycled glass. Vetrazzo uses glass gleaned from all types of sources—from broken traffic lights to plain cracked windows—captured in an inert base of cement and other natural additives. The glass pieces are clearly visible, and the countertops come in many different colors.

is an expensive option that should only be attempted by knowledgeable and experienced pros. And you'd better love the look, because replacing a concrete countertop is no small task.

COUNTERTOP COMPLEMENTS

Backsplashes are your chance to accent the kitchen design without spending a whole lot of money, time, or effort. I look at them as small, wide, blank canvases on which you can exercise your creativity. Formed countertops (such as solid-surface) often come with a 2- or 3-inch-high backsplash molded into the countertop. That's fine on a practical level and there's no crime in leaving it at that. But you can do so much more with the space.

Simply tiling the wall between the countertop and the bottom of the cabinets offers nearly endless design possibilities. A super chic span of monochromatic glass tiles would be right at home in a modern kitchen, while a collection of hand-painted ceramic tiles brings an enchanting detail to a country kitchen. There's just no end to the potential design accents you can create given the amazing selection of tiles available.

YOU CAN . . . Make Your Own Unique Backsplash

Sure, creating a backsplash from tiles can be hugely rewarding. But why not go even more original? You can create a personalized backsplash using castable resin and personal keepsakes or pictures. Simply coat whatever items you want to display with resin sealer, place them in the mold (molds, resin, and other materials can be purchased at craft stores), and pour the resin over them. Use a square or rectangular mold to create resin "tiles" for the backsplash. Once the resin cures, the tiles can be drilled for mounting, or can be stuck to a white-painted backsplash wall with a special clear adhesive.

A glass tile backsplash is a sensual addition to a kitchen, inviting to the eyes as well as the hands. The surface also amplifies light in the room, and the variety of colors available is astounding.

You'll find an incredible selection of specialty tiles—like these black "rock" glass tiles—to dress up your backsplash.

Solid backsplashes are another great option. A stainless steel surface behind an onyx or black marble countertop makes for a show-stopping combination. Copper squares introduce a cool touch in a cottage kitchen. Pressed tin, like the sheets used to restore period tin ceilings, serves the same purpose (although you need to seal the sheets to make them cleanable).

Super Sinks and Faucets

Choosing a sink—and faucet—goes hand in glove with choosing a countertop. Your sink is ultimately going to have to fit an opening in a countertop and, if you have chosen a solid-surface countertop, your sink will likely be molded right into it. Swapping out a sink is also a quick and easy way to change the look of your kitchen. In any case, always consider sink depth—shallow sinks are harder to work in and fill up with dishes much quicker than deeper units do.

As with your countertops, choosing a sink begins with choosing a material. Stainless steel sinks are the most popular, and they are suitable to almost any kitchen design. They are also durable and great for cleanup of hot or cold cookware. However, you should buy at least an 18-gauge sink or the surface may flex and dent.

Porcelain-glazed cast-iron sinks are also well-liked for their sheer durability and handsome appearances. The porcelain surface can be tinted in many different colors, although white remains the most popular because it works with any design scheme. The drawback to cast-iron sinks is that they are heavy and hard to install, and the porcelain coating is susceptible to chipping and cracking—a consideration if you clean a lot of heavy pots and pans.

Stainless steel sinks (top) are the most popular choice for kitchens, for good reason. They are easy to clean, stand up to hot pots and pans and substances such as grease, and don't chip, fade, or otherwise degrade over time and use. The double bowl design is one of the most popular styles. A newer option, engineered stone surfaces such as this double-bowl design (bottom), offers a unibody sink that is durable, handsome, easy to clean, and available in several different colors and many different sizes and bowl configurations.

Stone is an unusual choice and a distinctive look. The price is also distinctively high. Consider a stone sink only if you're absolutely set on the look and feel—because the look can be replicated to a fair degree in a cheaper, easier-to-install, solid-surface material such as Corian.

Acrylic sinks are inexpensive and lightweight, making them easy to handle and install. They are also sealed surfaces that resist scratches and stains and are available in a painter's palette of colors. However, they are susceptible to cracking and damage from heat—a real drawback for a surface that will likely be exposed to boiling water and cookware just removed from burners. That's why I shy away from using acrylic sinks.

Shape will be another consideration. Kitchen sinks are most commonly rectangular, although square and, more rarely, circles and ovals can be found as well. The more important factor is the number of bowls. Separate, side-by-side bowls allow you to wash and rinse cookware and dishes, or prep food in one bowl while washing up in another. Choose the number of bowls that will accommodate how you cook, prep, and wash dishes.

The actual sink measurements are important. The size needs to leave room in front of and behind the sink for a countertop lip (unless the sink is a farmhouse or apron-style sink, in which the front of the sink is left exposed). Sink depth is a crucial measurement, affecting how useful the sink will be. Deeper sinks allow you to manipulate large pots and pans easily for cleaning. Although it may be tempting to buy the deepest sink you can find, keep in mind that installing or replacing a faucet means getting up behind the sink, something that can be made a lot more difficult with a deep sink. You'll also need to be sure there is room under the sink to make essential connections to the dishwasher and garbage disposal, if you have either or both of those.

Mounting style is a matter of taste and, depending on what type of sink you choose, may be predetermined. Kitchen sinks are mounted in one of three ways: top, flush, or undermount. Top-mounted sinks are easiest to install because they drop right into place, resting on a lip built into the sink. The lip edge can catch dirt and debris, but this is the only type of sink that can be used with laminate countertops, because the other types leave the counter edge exposed.

Flush-mounted sinks create a sleek, seamless look that, like undermount sinks, allows for easy clean up (you can wipe the counters right into the sink). Flush-mounted sinks are usually used with tiled countertops. Undermount sinks are positioned below the bottom of the counter and are the hardest to install.

They are most often used with stone or other solid-surface countertops.

The sink you choose needs to be paired with a faucet. This should be easy because there are so many faucet styles and finishes, including brushed nickel, chrome, copper, brass, and enamel-coated in several basic colors. You can also choose from two-handled faucets and those with a single handle on the body. The look you select should be driven by how well the faucet matches the sink, cabinet hardware, and lighting fixtures. The number of handles and other features are really a matter of personal preference. But one feature I'd strongly recommend you consider is a pull-out spray head, which can make kitchen clean-up much easier.

Storage in Style

Kitchen and dining rooms never seem to have enough storage. A redesign is your chance to fix that situation. Kitchen cabinets are the place to start, because they hold so much of what you will use in both the kitchen and dining room. You may be perfectly happy with the placement and capacity of your current cabinets, and that's fine. I work with a lot of home-owners who prefer to keep their existing cabinets, rather than go to the expense of replacing them. But keeping your cabinets doesn't mean you have to keep the look of the cabinets.

Your solid wood cabinets may be a little worse for the wear, making them prime candidates for painting or refinishing. It's a lot of labor and it should be done carefully, but refinishing cabinets is something you can do without much skill or equipment, and it makes the whole kitchen look new. It's as simple as sanding the wood (just down to a stable surface if you're painting, all the way down to bare wood if you're staining or finishing natural), and applying the paint, stain, or finish. Unless I'm staining cabinets a shade that should be left flat, I always use high-gloss paint or polyurethane as a topcoat. This ensures the surfaces are extremely easy to clean and amplifies the light in the space.

A finely detailed storage piece such as this Craftsman-style sideboard brings big flair to a dining room design. It also offers a wealth of hidden and exposed storage, and a top surface that can be used to hold plates of food during special meals.

Light brown maple cabinets go perfectly with eco-friendly recycled paper countertops and stone tile backsplashes. The eye-pleasing blend of natural tones in this kitchen creates a warm, inviting look.

If you're painting the cabinets, the color possibilities are wide open. Complement the color scheme you've already established, or set the tone for the scheme you want. However, if your cabinets are solid wood, give some serious consideration to letting handsome wood grain speak for itself. A natural wood finish is the perfect partner to a subtle contemporary or traditional kitchen design. Ebony stain makes more of a modern statement. You can use other stain colors to give the wood grain the red hue of mahogany or the deep brown of oak—whatever suits the other colors in the kitchen.

Not everyone is lucky enough to have solid-wood cabinets. Your cabinets may be laminates—essentially particleboard boxes with wood or other veneer glued over the faces and doors. That doesn't mean you should run out and buy new cabinets. If you like the shape, location, and capacity of your cabinets, you can simply reface them. Refacing involves removing the existing veneer from the frame and exposed sides of the cabinets, and applying new veneer in its place. The cabinet doors are often replaced as part of a refacing project, and it gives you the opportunity to switch to flat, raised-panel, or recessed-panel doors, whichever suits the overall decor and your tastes. You can also substitute glass-front doors for all or some of the cabinets. Whether you reface the cabinets yourself (requires a sharp utility knife, patience, and an eye for exacting detail) or have a pro do it, the cost will be a fraction of what new cabinets would run you. And the result is a clean, entirely new look. You can reface with wood-grain veneers or laminate veneers in a wide selection of colors and patterns.

Sometimes, though, a facelift is not enough. You may want to completely change the style, location, or number of cabinets, which can only mean new units. Start your search by deciding between the two basic cabinet styles—frameless and framed. Framed cabinets are built with a nonstructural frame attached to the front of the box. The door sits inside or in front of the frame, but the frame shows. Frameless cabinets lack this feature—the door sits inside the front edges of the cabinet box, or covers them entirely. Frameless cabinets are a more streamlined and modern look. Framed cabinets are the traditional and conventional look. Frameless cabinets are usually fronted with flat doors or, less often, doors with recessed panels. Framed cabinets are usually equipped with doors with raised panels. Once you've settled on the box and door styles that suit your kitchen best, choose a wood and finish—or synthetic veneer—that captures the color and patterns you want.

A suite of framed cabinets brings a classic style to this kitchen, and one that complements the stunning marble floor and island top, and the stainless steel appliances.

A mix of cabinet finishes gives this kitchen a blast of design flair. The taupe bottom cabinets fit right into the room's neutral color scheme, and the frosted glass cabinet fronts capture much of the magic of clear glass fronts, but without the need to keep everything in the cabinets looking neat. Hanging storage and custom shelf units round out a super functional and stylish kitchen.

Regardless of the type of cabinets, I like to use glass fronts as the budget allows. They really add a special element. But as much as I like them, I only include them on cabinets in which something attractive will be stored. Glass fronts revealing a jumble of cereal boxes and potato chip bags are a waste of money—and detract from the design at large—as far as I'm concerned. Picking and choosing which cabinet doors get glass fronts means knowing what you're going to store where. But frankly, you should figure that out before you pick out cabinets in any case. I use glass fronts for cabinets that hold attractive stemware like wine glasses, or decorative bowls.

One last word on glass fronts, though: Not all glass is created equal. As if you didn't have enough choices to make, you can select plain glass for your cabinet doors, or choose from many other types. Textured glass comes in different looks, many that obscure what's inside the cabinet and provide a graphic detail worthy of attention in its own right. A slightly bigger budget opens up your potential choices to include frosted glass, stained glass, and beveled glass partitions. Just be sure that whatever glass treatment you decide on doesn't clash with the style of the cabinet itself.

Cabinet hardware is, like drawer pulls and countertop accents, jewelry for the kitchen. New door pulls, handles, and hinges won't break the bank, and they are details that add visual appeal far out of proportion to their small sizes. The hardware should reinforce the cabinet style (for example, ornate handles with traditional cabinets, sleek silver pulls and hinges on modern frameless units in a European kitchen). I always advise homeowners to consider hardware choices in relation to fixtures like lights and faucets. If those fixtures are all brushed pewter and your door hardware is shiny chrome, you may create a jarring contrast.

CARTER'S LAW:
Exploit Your Kitchen Storage

Most of the storage in a kitchen is hidden behind the doors of your cabinets. Even so, it can affect the overall design by reducing the amount of space you need for storage furniture, such as sideboards or stand-alone cabinets. Effective storage also reduces clutter, making the kitchen easier to work in and more attractive. Make the most of your cabinet storage by looking beyond plain shelves. Corner cabinets are much more accessible when they're fitted with lazy Susan shelves that spin for ultimate access. Buy adjustable versions to retrofit existing cabinets, or order them as a feature in new cabinetry. Save a lot of bending and stooping with slide-out shelves, especially handy in deep cabinets. I go with slide-out drawer shelves whenever possible—the sides keep everything contained and the drawer looks sharp when you open the cabinet. Simple organizers like spice "stadium" shelves or adjustable shelves can help bring order to a cabinet or a whole pantry. Go for the extra effort and modest expense to step up from plain shelves, and you'll never regret it.

Pull-out trash or recycling bins are a great solution for keeping mess out of sight in a well-designed kitchen.

Hinged, pull-out shelves are ideal for making the most of cramped corner cabinets, top or bottom.

Getting your cabinet choices squared away is no small feat, but once you've decided on the cabinet types, door styles, surfacing, and hardware, you will have finalized a major piece of your kitchen design, and one that drives many other decisions. The next step is to figure out how to shine the right light on that design.

DEEP GREEN CHOICES: Cabinet Recycling Bins

Did you know that Americans only recycle 35 percent of household waste? We can do much better than that. At my wedding, we ended up with only half a bag of trash because we composted and recycled everything else. That's why as part of any kitchen redesign I work on, I push for built-in and removable recycling and compost bins. These are big plastic bins in a simple wood or metal frame, mounted on sliding tracks that are screwed to the side or bottom of the cabinet (usually the large space under a kitchen sink). They make it easy to collect cans or paper in one convenient location, rather than throwing them out. The compost side is even more important, because most of what we throw out is organic waste. Collect everything but fats and proteins like meat in the compost bin, and then take it outside when it's full and dump it in your composter if you have one. If you don't, you can make a simple compost pile in a corner of the yard or flowerbed—just empty the bin on the ground and turn the pile every week or so to create a great garden amendment. You'll be doing your garden a favor and helping the environment at the same time.

Who says composting can't be stylish? This in-counter stainless steel composting bin holds kitchen waste in high style and is easy to use. This particular unit is available as a slide-in insert and a flush-mount version. Either can be retrofitted to an existing counter and both are easy to clean.

Light It Right

You've carefully chosen just the right decorative elements for your kitchen or dining room. You've followed the design style you established in the first place, know what colors you'll use and what the overall look will be. But all that effort will be greatly diminished if you don't light the room to its best advantage.

Lighting kitchens and dining rooms can be a challenge, because the spaces play different roles at different times. The kitchen is especially complex. Lighting specialists like to talk about "layering" lighting in the kitchen. What they mean is providing different types of lighting for different purposes. The ideal kitchen lighting scheme depends on the space and how it's used. But the single overhead light that marked kitchens of the past simply doesn't get the job done.

Your general lighting will usually be supplied by a mix of fixtures. If the redesign includes some renovation, I look to install recessed ceiling lights. A cluster, row, or circle of recessed lights produces a soft, clean, and diffused general-purpose light that not only illuminates the whole space fairly evenly but also creates a

Recessed ceiling lights provide the ambient light for this kitchen, but that's just a start. Pendants over the island (the most common type of island lights) provide strong lighting for food prep and eating. Undercabinet lights keep countertop areas shadow-free even during the day, and an accent light plays up the elegance of the glass cabinet fronts.

nice mood. I like to use adjustable recessed lights whenever possible, because flexibility is key in lighting a kitchen (or any room for that matter).

Even if the budget doesn't allow for cutting up the ceiling and wiring in recessed lights, I expand on the overhead lighting that is there. Track lights come in many different styles and allow you to upgrade to more versatile and adjustable lighting that can be wired into existing fixture boxes. Although it's not my first choice for the kitchen, track lighting can be pretty handy because it's so easy to point the individual fixtures exactly where you want the light to go. Plus, the styles cover the whole gamut of kitchen designs, from sleek modern and high-tech units to plain white fixtures that would blend right into the ceiling of a traditional or contemporary room. The point is, switching to a multifixture general overhead light source is a must in my book.

But don't stop there. Next up is your task lighting. You need to see what you're doing when you're working with knives, pointy utensils, and power appliances. The right work lighting is key to how comfortable your kitchen will be for prepping and cooking. Look to eliminate shadows that make prepping and cooking harder. The sink should have its own light source, whether it's a recessed light or a pendant.

Undercabinet lighting is your best friend when it comes to working in the kitchen. Again, use as many fixtures as necessary to eliminate shadows on the countertop. This usually means spacing individual fixtures no more than 20 inches apart. The best undercabinet lighting is wired in and sits flush, so that it is hidden in the shallow cavity under the cabinet. However, your project may not allow for new wiring, in which case you can find very discreet plug-in or battery-powered undercabinet fixtures.

Islands also need their own lighting. The current vogue is to use pendants, which are ideal for this role—regardless of whether the island is used for cooking, prep, cleanup, dining, or all of the above. There are

As far as I'm concerned, undercabinet lighting is a must-have in the kitchen; it makes the work surfaces safer and easier to use and helps create an inviting mood. You can use simple battery-powered fixtures mounted to the underside of your cabinets, or go more high-tech with a solution like these modern, rail-mounted, stainless steel fixtures.

pendants in just about every design style imaginable, with more on the market every day.

A lot of today's kitchen designers are enchanted with kitchen accent lights. These are meant to provide additional decorative lighting—such as uplights concealed on top of cabinets that don't run all the way to the ceiling, and interior lights for glass-fronted cabinets. Personally, I think a well-lit kitchen with a mix of task and general lighting is just fine as it is. But if you want to add a little sparkle, by all means accent your kitchen lighting scheme.

The kitchen table should have its own light, and it's possible that there is already an overhead fixture above it. But if there's not, you should absolutely add one. Today's kitchen table—like today's kitchen—is used for many different purposes. At one moment, a family member may be working on a computer, while the next, you might be playing a board game with friends. A fairly bright hanging light or ceiling fixture—on a dimmer or a three-way fixture—answers all those needs admirably. Because these are some of the most popular types of lighting, you'll find a slew of choices at the local home center.

In most dining rooms, a hanging fixture is centered over the table—or the table is centered under the hanging fixture. A

A formal dining room is almost always lit by a formal "candle-style" chandelier. It's a classic look, but chandeliers come in just about every style imaginable, from Spanish Mission style through modern. The fixture style should match the table and chairs.

chandelier is the traditional fixture, but what constitutes a chandelier has changed over time. Although your dining room may call for the conventional ornate chandelier with curving arms and faux candle bulbs, there are so many other designs from which to choose. Think of a material and a chandelier has most likely been made from it. Wrought iron, hardwood, glass, even resin have all been pressed into service to sculpt the dining room's main light fixture. Pick one that meets your budget and complements the design. However, practicality also needs to play a part in your choice. The sum of the wattages in a multilight fixture mustn't exceed the wattage of the electrical circuit to which the light is connected.

Complement an overhead dining room light with fill sources such as sconces. Uplight or downlight sconces can add a touch of drama to a dining room. Stand-alone light fixtures have no place in the kitchen, but they are certainly wonderful additions to the dining room. Torchieres or simple standing lamps can provide fill lighting to brighten a corner of the room, and the same is true of a lamp on a sideboard.

The key—whether you're lighting a kitchen or a dining room—is to provide enough supplemental lighting to fill in, and prevent distracting and troublesome shadows. Only with the right mix of lighting will the design really come to life, particularly the less noticeable but still important little accents that help define your signature style.

Furnishing for Dining

Both the kitchen and dining room are all about the table and chairs. I can't tell you the number of homes I've visited in which the owners have suffered for years with the wrong size or shape of kitchen or dining room table. It's just one of those small irritations that we quickly accept—our chair will bang the wall, people will struggle to move around the table when other people are seated there, and the whole room is difficult to clean because the table is always in the way. Don't put up with a table that doesn't work.

That's not to say that every kitchen and dining room table needs to be replaced. Your table and chairs may be perfectly suited to your space and decorative style. But even if you're going to keep the table and chairs you have, look at them through fresh eyes—maybe even a friend's. A scratched or dingy finish will clash with the other elements in your newly redesigned kitchen or dining room, and torn seat cushions aren't anybody's idea of chic. If you're faced with refinishing a table, look at it as an opportunity, the chance to create a distinctive focal point where once there was a frumpy piece of furniture. Alternating stripes of color or shades of stain can turn a square or rectangular table into a conversation piece. Don't be afraid to play off the larger design. For instance, a round kitchen table with a high-gloss red finish might be a stunning counterpoint in a largely black-and-gray kitchen design.

The dining room suite you choose should depend not only on your style, but also on the pieces you need based on how you will use your dining room. Here, a stately Brazilian cherry wood floor serves as the stage for a contemporary table and matching hutch and sideboard. The room features ample storage for just about anything that might be needed for a dinner party.

A round kitchen table such as this is not only an adaptable shape that fits comfortably in many different plans, it also fosters intimacy and conversation because everyone faces everyone else.

On the other hand, if your table simply doesn't suit the space, or is too dinged up or too cheap to merit refinishing, head to the nearest furniture store. Choose shape and size first. Obviously, you can pick from a circle, square, or rectangle. Circular tables work best in a square space, where traffic flow is a key concern. They are most often used in kitchens, and rarely in dining rooms. Rectangular tables are ideal in long narrow spaces and are the shape of choice for most dining rooms because the corners allow more room for extra diners or to place dishes of food. Square tables work best in square spaces, although they also fit well in the odd-shaped corners of an eat-in kitchen.

Whichever shape you choose, buy an adjustable table. Some incorporate guides to slide one section of the table under another, but the most useful come with multiple leaves that are inserted into the table. This allows you to more than double the table's surface area at a moment's notice. For smaller spaces in kitchens, I like to use round tables with fold-down leaves that allow one side to fit flush up against a wall.

This is one of the reasons I'm just a little leery of glass tables. Not only are they generally not adjustable, they are also difficult to keep clean, and many people find eating on a glass surface disconcerting because of the confusing visual depth. If the look appeals to you, consider one with a frosted top that offers a more sophisticated appearance.

Your choice of table may also be affected by leg position. A center pedestal allows for the most flexibility in positioning people around the table. But center-pedestal supports are generally limited to round and small tables. More often than not, you'll be looking at tables with four legs. Where those legs fall determines how comfortable the table will be to sit at. Legs at the corners offer the most leeway for tucking in extra chairs. The closer the legs are to the center of the table, the more likely they are to interfere with a seated person's legs.

When you have some idea of the style of table you're after, start looking for the perfect candidate. Take along your measurements and a measuring tape to prevent surprises when you get

An elegant dining table and chairs and sideboard are often all the furniture you need . . . especially in a bold, contemporary room design such as this one.

your table home. It's also a good idea to bring along paint chips or color swatches so that you don't choose a table finish that clashes with the design you've established, or stands out like a sore thumb.

I don't believe in adding furniture—beyond the table and chairs—to a kitchen. Cabinetry and wall-mounted shelves should supply all your storage. Any other furnishings tend to get in the way in this high-traffic room. The more area you can leave to move around in, the better.

Dining rooms, however, are often well served by pieces that complement the table and chairs. Go vertical in a smaller dining room, with a tall shallow hutch or bar unit. These can be great places to store—and even display—crystal, china, and hallmark serving pieces. When you have the space of a larger dining room, consider adding a console table or sideboard. Either of these low-slung pieces brings a splash of style to the room and, on the functional side, they provide both storage and a spot to sit food during meals.

I always tell homeowners to choose secondary dining room furnishings that maintain the style established by the table and chairs. For instance, in a formal dining room with detailed crown molding, wainscoting, and a fancy dining room set, I'd choose a hutch and a sideboard with the ornate detailing and darker surface finish. A squared off, blockier style would better suit a plain contemporary dining room outfitted with a streamlined and elegant table and chairs. In short, dining room secondary pieces should be there because they serve your storage needs, and they should provide further indicators of the style you're after.

Icing on the Cake

We are never finished with a kitchen or dining room redesign on one of my shows until we've added the accents. These are the small touches that complete the design and allow you to put your signature on it. I find the most successful accents combine style and function. Accents are the difference between just a room and a finished, well-designed room. For instance, wine racks are just about essential in a dining room or kitchen. Unless you don't drink and don't throw parties, having a few nice bottles of wine on hand is one way to always be ready for entertaining, and they just look great.

The wonderful thing about wine racks is that they come in so many styles and sizes. A wine buff can choose a larger wooden box unit to hold a case of bottles at a time. Someone who enjoys the occasional glass of vino can opt for a much smaller rack for three bottles. Regardless of the size, the style options are incredible. I've seen wood box racks stained light and dark (I've made a couple of these, but they're harder than they first appear), and you can even paint them to suit your decor.

Riding the vast popularity of hanging pot racks, hanging rails offer wall-mounted storage with accessories for everything from spice racks to utensil storage to paper towel dispensers. As this kitchen clearly shows, the look is attractive and makes the most hardworking room in the house easier to use.

The most popular wine racks are metal. Iron makes for a great look in a Mediterranean-style kitchen, while a curvy metal rack is right at home in a traditional dining room. There are neat, stream-lined styles that are essentially a vertical piece with holes in it, in which the bottle necks are placed so that gravity holds the bottles in place. You'll find the greatest number of options online or in catalogs. Whichever style catches your eye, I'd suggest you consider a wall-mounted version. It's the rare kitchen or dining room where floor and counter space are not at a premium.

One of the terrific things about a kitchen is that so many of the tools of the trade are attractive in their own right. This gives

you the chance to store in plain sight, and use utilitarian objects as decorative accents. Pot racks are a prime example. Where the ceiling is high enough, a hanging pot rack screams "cook's kitchen" and—depending on the type of pots and pans—you'll be adding wonderfully attractive elements to the room's design. Knife holders are another way to exploit practical items for decorative purposes. I prefer to use magnetic strips rather than the traditional wood blocks, which have been found to harbor bacteria if not kept scrupulously clean.

Beyond getting your gear out in the open, you can also display food staples, although I'm less enthusiastic about incorporating food into the kitchen's design. Unless you're an avid cook who uses a lot of ingredients every day, fruit and vegetables stored in baskets look good for a day or two until they begin to rot. Spice racks are a particular look best suited to a country-style or traditional kitchen, although you can find high-tech and modern looking versions (I've seen test-tube spice racks, and metal spice jars that are arranged on a wall-hung magnetic stainless-steel plate). I'd suggest you use a spice rack only if you're going to use the spices regularly. Otherwise it's ornamentation for ornamentation's sake, which usually adds up to needless visual clutter.

Accenting a dining room is more about mood than showing off utilitarian objects. Candlesticks or candelabras look great in just about any style of dining room, partly because there are candlesticks in every design style and every material imaginable. Taper candles are an elegant look right for any dining room, but I usually like to put them on a sideboard during meals; tall candles in the middle of a table can interfere with communication and interaction among people at the table. Candelabras are best suited to more formal dining rooms where you want to inject a little drama into the look.

Vases and decorative platters can make for really nice accents in a dining room or larger kitchen with a clearly separate dining area. I like vases because they add shape, color, and texture to the room with little effort or expense. They look great when used just as sculptural elements in a group or as a focal point, and they look even more spectacular filled with seasonal cut flowers.

The right platter or decorative basket can add as much as a vase would to a dining room, and can be used to hold rolls, crudités, or other appropriate foods. Always look for your dining room accents to do double duty whenever possible.

With your design accents in place, all that's left is to invite some friends over, open a bottle of wine to breathe, and start preparing a meal to celebrate your newly redesigned space.

Chapter 3
SPECIAL, RESTFUL SPACES

I think of bedrooms as unique rooms in a house. Most other spaces are common areas, used by guests and family alike. Bedrooms, though, are all about who sleeps there. Your bedroom should be an ideal sanctuary where you can shut the world out and recharge.

This bedroom embodies luxury in all the sensuous textures—from rich bed linens, to the wicker furnishings, to the elegant drapes. Individual adjustable bedside lamps and wall-to-wall carpeting complete the look of a room that just invites enjoying the feel of fibers.

Great bedroom design invites rest and relaxation and promotes sound sleep and intimacy. It also looks sharp even in artificial light. That translates to a great bed and bedding, furniture and a layout that beat clutter by design, and surfaces that are a pleasure to all your senses. Comfort is king in the bedroom.

Comfort begins with the bed, and so does the room's style. Mattresses and bedding are important, and bedding will play a role in the look of the room. For now, though, let's start with the structure underneath all that.

Why We Call It the *Bed*room

The eight or more hours a night we spend getting some shut-eye makes the bed the most used piece of furniture in the house. It's also one of the biggest, which is why it's the centerpiece of the bedroom. There are many bed styles, but any bed you choose must be proportional to room size and the other furnishings.

The most basic beds are just an iron rail frame, boxspring, mattress, and a simple headboard. Headboards come in just about any style. The great thing about a basic metal frame bed is that it takes up little room and doesn't cost much. They're great for guest rooms and for kids, but most homeowners want a bit more style in a main bedroom.

There's a big trend these days toward platform beds. The look is streamlined and the bed doesn't require a boxspring, saving you money. Measure available space whenever you're thinking about a platform bed. Most have lips that often go all the way around

YOU CAN . . . Create Your Own Unique Headboard

A plain metal bed frame and mattress set may be functional, but it leaves something to be desired in the style department. Spruce up that simple look with a new or recycled panel door. Mounted sideways, these doors make interesting and unique headboards that you can finish to match the room's style. A new coat of paint, a distressed surface, or stripping and finishing the door in natural wood tones present all kinds of design possibilities. Hang the door with any of the vast number of hardware options available at hardware stores and home centers. You can buy panel doors new, but why not recycle and save a little money by picking one up at a salvage yard or reclaimed building goods supplier? It's the earth-friendly way to make your bed look super smart.

A stunning orange and black color scheme makes a bold, contemporary design statement in this well-appointed bedroom. The platform bed fits right into the dynamic style, part of a fashionable suite of furnishings.

the bed, adding several inches or more to the outside dimension (you always want to maintain at least 24-inch-wide traffic lanes in a bedroom). The same holds true for traditional sleigh beds, with their S-profile footboards and headboards. They can take up a lot more room than you might think when you're looking at them in a showroom.

Other beds, such as a poster or canopy, take up vertical room. Measure the height of your bedroom ceiling and the height of the bed's posts. A bed that has only a couple inches to spare between post and ceiling inevitably looks wedged into the room; 5 inches or more is usually the best look. Think carefully about a fancier bed, because beds last a long time; an ornate design like a poster bed may not be the look you want in two or three years, especially if you change houses in that time. I find it's safest to choose a general style that fits the room design you want to create, and then lean toward a simpler version of that style.

Carter's Case Study:
The Volkmann Bedroom

Corey Volkmann and her husband Joel Hawke had simply run out of decorating energy by the time my crew came on the scene. To their credit, they had remodeled most of the house Corey had grown up in, establishing their own eclectic-slash-modern style. They had even turned a second bedroom into a presentable walk-in closet.

The problem was the master bedroom. They knew what they wanted, but Joel had started traveling every week for work, leaving precious little time or energy to complete the project. A foot-wide strip of laminate flooring remained to be laid along one side of the bedroom, the paint on the walls was a first effort that the couple didn't like, and the bed was a particular irritation to Corey. She told me, "I want a real bed. Not a metal frame."

Corey and Joel had a great vision for the room—a stylish, private hideaway where they could enjoy each other's company and watch TV and movies. They had even tried to convert the unused closet into an entertainment center. "Tried" being the operative word; the pre-fab closet inserts made for a partial design, a tumble of cords was still visible, and remnants of the ugly green carpet that once covered the floor remained.

The couple had the right idea in turning an unused closet into a home theater, but the project needed a bit more design work and execution.

The bed area was a blank canvas. The unfinished flooring can be seen along the wall at the right.

Once we cleared the room of furniture—including stripping out the closet structures—it was clear that the room had lots of potential. We settled on a sophisticated, modern, muted gray for the walls, with an accent wall of bright yellow facing the door, against which the bed's headboard would be placed.

It's not normally a great idea to use a bold or warm color in a bedroom. The room is supposed to be restful, and those colors are anything but. That said, an accent wall is an easy way to add some zip to the design. By placing it behind the bed, we made sure the couple wouldn't wake up or go to sleep facing a pulse-quickening blast of color. We also decided to cover the bottom half of the accent wall with a wall-to-wall headboard. Corey loved the idea because she longed for a stylish bed. To give her that, we decided to build a platform to match the headboard.

Designer Jinnie Choi painted the room with Corey and Joel chipping in, and we were ready to install the headboard and bed. Joel helped me frame the headboard using sections of 8-inch MDF (medium density fiberboard) planks as studs. I used longer sections for the bottom and top plates. I love to use MDF on projects like this; it's the ideal choice for quick and easy structures that won't see a lot of wear and tear. It's easy to work with, comes in several different sizes, and is fairly inexpensive. Mistakes won't set you back an arm and a leg.

We also added some cool lighting to the headboard. I drilled holes for wires at regular intervals along the top plate and we installed "puck" uplights to provide drama and highlight the accent wall. I used low-voltage pucks because they're a green choice that consume a lot less energy than standard puck lights. We finished the headboard with MDF facing panels painted high-gloss black. The black was the perfect complement to the yellow and gray, and really drove home the modern vibe.

Carpenter Jake Scott built the bed frame from the same MDF we used for the headboard. He assembled a box-frame base, topped with two 4-foot by 8-foot MDF panels for the platform. We painted the facing and platform gloss black and the bed area really began to take shape. Always keep in mind that you don't necessarily have to buy a new piece of furniture; the bed and headboard took us all of about a day, and it required very modest DIY skills!

I wanted two bedside tables to take up minimal room and maintain the spacious, modern feeling we were after. I cut two MDF panels about a foot square, and covered the surface with zebrawood veneer. A black edge banding on three sides finished the shelves, and I mounted them in place on either side of the bed with black brackets that couldn't be seen unless you kneeled and looked under the shelves. That made them seem to float—a very hip look perfect for a modern room design.

The next piece of the puzzle was the entertainment center. The empty closet was the right place for it, but it really called for custom cabinetry to create a polished look. Tapping Corey to help me, I built some basic box cabinets for top and bottom. Custom cabinet work like this is much simpler than it might appear. You can do it yourself if you use high-quality wood, measure twice, and cut once (the carpenter's way of saying, "be careful and methodical"). The cabinets were constructed with "butt" joints, in which the ends are simply butted together, glued, and screwed in place to form the boxes. I made doors from the same lumber, applying zebrawood veneer on the bottom doors and mirrored acrylic on the top. I added basic piano hinges on the top cabinets, but used barrister hinges on the bottom, which have rails and allow the doors to be opened and then slid back inside the cabinet. It's a very sleek look. Although the entertainment center cabinetry required precise measuring and cutting, it didn't call for super high-end carpentry skills. Take your time and be careful, and you could create the same cabinets for your home.

Jinnie Choi finished the entertainment center design by covering the zebrawood veneer with a plastic film. She cut a flowing organic design out of the plastic and removed that part of the film. She spray-painted the areas over

The bed and headboard turned out fantastic. Notice the uplights that draw attention to both the accent wall and the flowing, wall-mounted art.

A little bit of minor carpentry created this seamlessly integrated media center, with a design that echoes the art over the bed.

which the plastic had been removed, creating an artsy flowing pattern on top of the zebrawood veneer. This is a simple technique most anyone could try—although I'd suggest you start out with easier geometric patterns, rather than the freehand abstract Jinnie created.

Jinnie replicated the cabinet door design in a larger version cutout of acrylic and spray-painted it a mottled silver. We mounted this as art above the bed's headboard. It's a great accent that ties both ends of the room together. Curving and flowing shapes help soften the hard lines of a modern design and bring a bit of unexpected flair to the modern-style room.

Jinnie added hanging lamps over the bedside tables. The tables would not have accommodated full-size table lamps, and the hanging lamps fit the room's style perfectly. Don't shy away from unconventional solutions like this. Sometimes, the best answer lies in looking at a fixture, piece of furniture, or room accent in a different way, outside the conventional wisdom.

We finished off the design with a new couch placed at the foot of the bed facing the entertainment center, a rug with a modern pattern, bedding in white and black, and new window treatments of thick white-and-black drapes layered to block out the sun on sleep-in mornings. A few accents, including splashes of yellow on the bed and couch, tied the whole design together and gave the Volkmanns the bedroom they had wanted for so long and perfectly complemented the rest of their modern eclectic home.

Positioning Your Bed

Whether you're picking out a whole new bed or keeping the one you have now, begin the room's layout by positioning the bed. Even if you are sticking with your existing bed, don't assume it's in the best position possible.

Play around with the bed's position. When I was ten, I pushed my bed all around my room to get just the right setup. I would

Bed positioning is as much an issue of good sleep as it is about effective layout. Often the best positioning is with the bed facing away from or perpendicular to windows. Here, the positioning is not as much an issue because floor-to-ceiling light-blocking drapes have been used.

brace my back against a wall and push the heavy bed and furniture with my feet. I had to resort to this because my siblings just got tired of helping me change my room around so much. You can save yourself the back pains by doing this on a room sketch with a cutout of the bed. Whichever way you do it, a half hour of your time will result in a bedroom layout that is more comfortable, easier to keep clean, and more restful.

Last, if you have a large enough bedroom, try positioning the bed diagonally in a corner. It can be a very cool look where space isn't an issue—especially in a long thin bedroom.

The Colorful Bedroom

Bedroom color schemes have traditionally been based on muted, lighter colors. Dark and dramatic color combinations can close in the space and make it seem a little oppressive, while bright, bold, or warm colors can bring an unnerving energy to what is supposed to be a restful space. That's tradition. The colors you actually settle on should reflect how you want to use the room and how you live your life. For instance, if your goal is a romantic, secluded cave where you can hide away with that special someone, dark and dramatic colors may be just your style.

Cool natural colors, such as light green and blue, are still favorites for the relaxing atmosphere they create. Ocean blue, periwinkle, or morning glory blue are all great overall colors for a restful and

A neutral bedroom doesn't necessarily mean a lack of excitement. The rich deep browns, elegant taupe, and sophisticated whites in this room combine to create a picture of luxury. It's a comforting, enveloping color scheme that is also classically timeless.

Finely detailed and elegant period-style furnishings define this bedroom, and the sophisticated color scheme reinforces that style. The analogous orange-and-green combination in the window panels keeps the room from becoming too somber and adds even more interest to an already interesting room.

relaxing bedroom, as are light sage or kale. I like to pair these types of cool colors with a white ceiling and bright white trim, which keep the whole space looking clean and fresh.

However, if you're the type of high-energy individual who wakes up raring to go and thinks sleeping in is a big waste of time, you may want to choose bedroom colors with zip. Reds may work for you (although even if you're sold on using red, I would temper it with a creamy beige or areas of much lighter red or an analogous red-orange).

Neutrals are okay for a bedroom, although not my first choice. If that's the direction you want to go, vary the neutrals with at least an accent wall in a much deeper or lighter color. An all-beige bedroom is what absence of style looks like. I feel the same way about an all-white bedroom; modern, yes, but it simply looks too antiseptic, cold, and unwelcoming.

Filling in the Bedroom Layout

Once you've settled on the perfect position for your bed and have an idea of where you're going with your color scheme, choose and position the rest of the furnishings in your room. Start by considering your storage and organization needs.

I know that seems to be an odd place to begin putting together a bedroom layout, but it's actually a logical starting point. That's because there is so much you need to store and organize in the bedroom (organize being the real key word!). Let's consider the dresser for example.

Almost every homeowner I've ever met thinks the dresser is an essential piece of furniture in the bedroom. But is it? Larger closets in newer homes, along with highly detailed prefab closet systems, make that a relevant question to ask. If you're planning on revamping your bedroom closet—and especially if only one person uses the room—a dresser may be unnecessary. It's your judgment call.

If you include one, it needs to match the style of the room design you have in mind, and it needs to be sized correctly for the room. This is the number-one problem with most of the bedrooms I go into when I'm working on my TV shows. The dresser is so often some hulking thing that the owners have carted along with them through three different homes. Sometimes, replacing a piece of furniture that is otherwise basically sound pays off in terms of overall room usability and enhancing a particular room's design.

Not only should a nightstand match the style of the bed, it needs to fit into the layout and be usable from the bed. Ideally, the top of the nightstand should be as close as possible to exactly the same height as the top of the mattress—as this nightstand is.

Nightstands are a slightly different case. I'm a believer that it's the rare bedroom that can do without nightstands. I only leave them out of a bedroom design if there simply isn't enough room (in which case your bed is probably the wrong size for the room).

As they do with all furnishings, practical considerations will affect your choice of nightstand. The top needs to hold what you want next to your bed comfortably. For most people, this means a lamp, clock, and, often, space enough for a magazine or book. Any drawers or shelves should also be used for what you need around the bed—remote controls, reading glasses, or medications. Last, and perhaps most important, the top of any nightstand you choose should be level with the top of your mattress.

Beyond the basic "bedroom suite," many people add a bench or other seating at the foot of the bed. This makes a lot of sense to me, but only if there is plenty of room to navigate around the piece. As long as it's not in the way, it's nice to have the extra seating to put on shoes or socks, and a steamer trunk or other enclosed bench structure can be an opportunity to add storage. It can be a great way to store larger items, such as seasonal bedding, where you can get at them quickly and easily.

Comfort Underfoot

A wood floor or faux-wood laminate is a fine choice for the bedroom, but most of the homeowners I talk to think carpet is the height of bedroom comfort and luxury. I'll admit that it's pretty wonderful to take your first steps in the morning on a soft, warm, cushiony surface. We eat and drink a lot less in the bedroom than we do in other rooms, so carpet is also a little safer from stains than it would be elsewhere in the house. All in all, it's no wonder carpet remains the most popular flooring choice for bedrooms.

Not all carpet is created equal, however. The feel and quality of a given carpet are determined first by its fiber (or combination

A highly distinctive and stately room design like this calls for an equally stately floor covering such as the dense wall-to-wall carpet. Rich colors and sophisticated furniture detailing go hand-in-hand with a lush surface underfoot.

of fibers), and then by the way the fibers are formed and used. Except for wool, all carpet fibers are synthetic. Even wool, though, is often combined with synthetics to give the carpet better stain and fade resistance.

NYLON

This material is considered the Cadillac of carpet fibers. Extremely tough and durable, nylon maintains its form better than any other fiber (which keeps the carpet looking new). It has a soft feel that comes at a high price—second only to pure wool. It is also slightly less resistant to soil and stains than other synthetic fibers.

The fun style of two brothers' bunk beds is complemented by the look of a flokati rug. The natural yellow color works with the deep blue dominant room color, and the feel of a flokati surface underfoot is as enjoyable as the look.

TRIEXTA

The new kid on the block, this polymer is created from corn. Many professionals think this is the "fiber of the future," because it's extremely cleanable, durable, and stain-resistant—more so than any other fiber. It is also as soft as nylon, the fabric it most resembles in price as well.

POLYESTER

Polyester costs less than nylon or Triexta, with an incredibly soft feel that a lot of people say beats other fibers. The downside is that polyester is not as durable, and pure polyester carpets don't last as long as carpets made of other fibers. However, the lesser traffic and lighter use of a bedroom mean that polyester is a good candidate for carpeting there. A somewhat rougher-feeling and less expensive version of polyester, known as PET polyester, is made partially from recycled plastic containers. It's a "green" option but, unfortunately, it's prone to "pilling" and shedding fuzz.

OLEFIN

Olefin is so tough it's used for commercial and indoor/outdoor carpets. That toughness comes at the sacrifice of a nice feel. The texture is rough and the fiber holds dirt so that pure olefin carpets can start to look dingy after a short time. It also doesn't pop back

YOU CAN . . . Select the Best Quality Carpet

Keep an eye out for the telltale signs of quality when you shop for a luxurious bedroom floor covering. (The same signs of quality can help you decide on remnants for other rooms as well.)

- A thick, tight, heavy backing. The heavier the backing, the more durable the carpet and the more pleasant it will feel underfoot.

- Pile density is a measure of how much yarn was used and how tightly it is packed in. The denser the pile, the better the carpet. The common test used to check good pile density is to hold a sample with the fibers up, and then bend the edges of the sample down. The less backing you see through the fibers, the better.

- Tuft twists are the number of times each fiber is twisted. Usually, the more twists, the longer the carpet will look new, and the better it is. Look for "heat set" twisted fibers, which have excellent shape-retention properties.

- Woven or tufted. Weaving is a superior method of carpet construction; tufted carpet is cheaper.

- Warranty length. Manufacturers back up quality carpets for a decade or more; lesser versions rarely last more than five years.

to its original form very well, which is why most olefin carpets are made with short looped fibers that hold up better to foot traffic. The one big plus of olefin is that it's the least expensive carpet fiber. I only use olefin carpets in very high traffic areas; I opt for more luxurious fibers in the bedroom.

WOOL

Wool tops the list of carpet fibers in terms of pure luxury. The feel under your hand or your foot is sensational, soft, and warm. Luxury always has its price and wool is no different; it's the most expensive carpet fiber. And although it is fire-resistant, it stains fairly easily and usually requires professional cleaning, making it a less-than-stellar choice for kids' rooms or anywhere a pet spends time. All that is why most carpets that use wool fibers blend them with 20 percent or more synthetic fibers to get the best of both worlds.

Pick the carpet fiber that works best for your circumstances, and you've gone a long way toward finding your ideal carpet. Now you just have to settle on a color and pile.

Pile is simply how the fibers are used and treated in the carpet. In looped-pile carpets, the fiber is left as it is woven or tufted, after being looped through the backing. Cut-pile carpet fibers are cut after the carpet is woven so that the fibers stand straight up and down. Carpets also come with a combination of cut and looped piles, and with piles cut or looped at different heights. Mostly that's going to affect appearance, so let's talk practicality.

Looped-pile carpets are generally more durable, especially those with short, dense loops. Cut pile can, however, be much more luxurious, simply because you can fit in more fibers when you cut them. The knock on cut-pile carpet is that it leaves marks when someone walks over the top. I've never found that to be a big drawback, but decide for yourself. The lushest feel underfoot in a bedroom is going to be a cut-pile carpet.

Carpet in a neutral color such as this is more likely to fit into the bedroom decor when it comes time for updating. No matter what the color scheme, though, the carpet is a luxury underfoot.

DEEP GREEN CHOICES: Air-Friendly Carpet

Carpet is not one of the more eco-friendly flooring options, but you can buy versions that are better than most. The big concern is unhealthy volatile organic compounds (VOCs) that are released right after installation—that typical "new carpet" smell is actually toxic fumes. Do yourself a favor and check the label on carpets you are considering. Look to see that the carpet has been tested by the Carpet and Rug Institute (CRI), as part of their Indoor Air Quality program. If you see the initials CRI inside a green house logo, that's your sign that the carpet is low-emission. Even so, it's wise to air any new carpet out for twenty-four hours before installation in a garage or covered on a deck. You can also promote healthy indoor air by choosing a felt pad rather than one made from styrene-butadiene rubber.

The best way to test out a carpet sample is to put it on the ground and step on it. You'll get a sense of how it feels and how it rebounds from being crushed. Judging carpet color is a little trickier. The lights in big home centers or carpet stores are inevitably brighter than in your bedroom. So it's always a good idea to bring home a carpet sample—it's not a small investment and you'll be living with it for a long time. Buy smart.

White and very light colors of carpeting show dirt more readily than darker colors. However, the lack of traffic in your bedroom means you can consider a lighter color that complements the room's color scheme. I avoid extremely light or dark carpet and trendy colors because the color tends to grow old long before the carpet does.

Closet Chic

The most important closets in the house are in your bedroom. A well-organized, logically put together closet saves you time and frustration, and keeps clutter out of the bedroom proper. A sloppy, half-hearted closet design does just the opposite. I never design a bedroom without thoroughly rethinking the closets.

I start by asking homeowners how they use the closet. Couples need a clear idea of how much space the man needs as opposed to what the woman needs (yes, she usually needs more). Evenly

One of the most efficient ways to configure a reach-in closet is by centering the design on a shelf-and-drawer column, as shown here. Hanging storage is placed on either side of the column, and the drawer units can often take the place of a dresser.

CARTER'S LAW:
Give Clothes Space

It's essential to allow the proper space for clothing and accessories in a closet. When clothes have enough room to breathe, they last longer and look better, and a well-organized closet makes it easier to get dressed.

- A closet must be at least 22 inches deep to properly accommodate hanging storage.

- Allow 45 inches for half-height hanging clothing, including suits, shirts, blouses, sportscoats, and short skirts.

- Allow 72 inches of vertical space for full-height clothing, including long coats and dresses.

- Allow 2 horizontal inches or more for any hanging garment. Crowding garments on a hanging pole can lead to wrinkles and structural damage to the clothing.

- Closet shelves are regularly 10 inches deep, but if you plan on storing hefty boxes or stacks of fluffy folded sweaters or blankets, I'd opt for 12-inch-deep shelves.

- Plan on 7 to 9 inches of shelf or rack width for each pair of shoes you intend to store. Store shoes toe in so that they are easier to grab when you need them.

divided closets rarely serve anyone's interests. Whether you're fitting clothes for two into the space or streamlining a closet all your own, the big decision is how much hanging storage you need.

Hanging storage is largely going to determine the configuration of your closet. Boxes, bins, shoes, and folded clothes can all go on many different types of shelves, but garments that have to be hung can only be hung in one way. You should actually measure the amount of hanging garments you have and add 10 to 15 percent to determine the space you'll need to dedicate to hanging rods in your new closet design. One of the biggest potential space savers in renovating a closet is stacking hanging rods to store stacked rows of shorter garments such as shirts, blouses, and pants draped over a hanger.

From there, you can design a closet to fit your needs. Make a quick sketch of how you want the closet to be configured. Don't worry about standardized measurements because you can usually find or customize whatever you need.

There are a number of great retailers to help with that. They supply closet units with shelving in all different materials, from the low-end coated wire, to high-end solid wood. I don't usually look to make a stunning statement with closet organizer systems, but I do prefer to use solid shelving and a mix of drawers, open shelves, boxes, bins, and specialized storage such as cubbies. The beauty of adding a couple drawers is that it can alleviate some of the burden of the dresser (and sometimes replace a dresser altogether), and there are many inexpensive specialized organizers that will bring order to your bedroom. You'll find inserts for holding belts, ties, jewelry, and more. I also look for specialized storage fixtures, including motorized tie holders. These small changes can have a big impact on making your life easier and keeping your bedroom in order.

One last word about closet organization: shoes. Control your shoe chaos with some sort of shoe-specific storage. These can be simple canted racks that slide under the hanging storage in your closet, special "shoe cubby" shelves, or even hanging pockets if you prefer. The point is to have a specific place to put shoes. The reality about well-organized closet space is that proper, specific storage leads behavior. In other words, if your shoes are a jumble on the bottom of your closet, you're more likely to just take off your shoes and leave them on the floor of the bedroom; if there doesn't

A curved corner hanging rod increases the storage space in any closet.

seem to be a logical place to put a blazer in among overcrowded hanging garments, it's more likely just to be draped over the foot of the bed or on a nearby chair. That's how clutter chaos starts.

Managing Bedroom Media

The closet isn't the only place in your bedroom that calls for order. Often, the most unruly area of a bedroom is wherever the TV and electronics have been placed. They aren't natural parts of the bedroom setup, so it's understandable that a TV, DVD player, cable box, or other electronics so often get plunked down on top of a dresser, creating a messy tumble of equipment and power cables.

I like to watch TV in bed too, but if you're going to include this fixture in your bedroom, it shouldn't be placed as an afterthought. Creating a good-looking entertainment center in the bedroom is easier now than ever, thanks to flat-panel TVs and lightweight and miniaturized components. Wall mount whatever you can, and install specific shelving or storage units for whatever you can't. Where you can't hide cables behind a dresser or other furniture,

Complete closet organizing systems such as the one shown here are designed to make the most efficient use of closet space. Stacked hanging rods, special shoe shelves, and drawers combine with bins and other containers to accommodate just about anything you need to store.

use conduit or some other method to collect and disguise them (you'll find more ideas about this in chapter 4, page 111).

Keep in mind that TVs are made to be viewed head on, not from below the sight line. When positioning a TV in the bedroom, I like to have someone actually lie down with his or her head propped up. Then I place the TV screen in direct line of sight with the person's eyes. Set up any sound system you install with the same focus on the bed.

Personalizing a Personal Retreat

Decorative accents are your chance to really hit the luxury button in your bedroom decor. Start with the walls. Simple wall art is best in a bedroom because it should serve as background to the textiles in the space—the bedroom is all about tactile comfort after all. On that note, never be afraid to hang tapestry or other textile art on bedroom walls. Fabric wall tiles can create the perfect soft and luxurious vertical accent surface that makes the bedroom even more sensuous. Personally, I stay away from decorative mirrors in the bedroom, because it's the last room in which you want light bouncing around and amplifying. The only mirror I use is the one over a dresser or vanity table.

I carry the tactile design focus through to my choice of window treatments. This is a room that begs for distinctive window panels. I like heavier drapes because you inevitably want to block out light in the bedroom at some point. Lined drapes are an especially good choice. Because the window area you'll be covering is usually fairly modest, I splurge on the fabric. Heavy dark green, blue, or black velvet panels are a great look for a single guy's bedroom, while silk drapes add an incredible visual to a couple's bedroom. Even if you prefer more modest window treatments, don't go boring. Linen and cotton curtains, and linen-cotton blends, are a plainer look that still add attractive texture. Spice up the look a little bit with darker bands or stripes on the curtains—or accent with valances or tie-backs.

Decorative pillows, a round mirror in a stylized frame, and tabletop accents really personalize this space and add even more flair to an already bold color scheme and high-end furnishings.

Mood Lighting

Lighting the bedroom is a balancing act that means providing enough light for the space to be comfortable and easy to navigate, yet not so much that the mood and ambiance of the room are spoiled. Let's start with the bedside. Bedside lighting is mandatory, whether you read in bed or not. Choose fixtures based on your bedtime routine. If you read before going to sleep, look for an adjustable-head fixture so that you'll be able to direct the light onto the page but away from your partner. Wall-mounted lights with telescoping arms and swivel heads are great choices for avid bed readers. However, if reading is not part of your routine, simple bedside table lamps should suit the purpose. They come in every style imaginable to match any decor.

Don't be afraid to go unconventional with bedside fixtures. Hanging lamps suspended over bedside tables serve the same purpose as table lamps but don't take up space on the nightstand. Regardless of which you choose, be sure that when lying down, bare bulbs are never in your field of view. Another requisite is that lighting be controlled from the bed. Getting up to turn off lights runs counter to the theme of comfort and luxury.

Your bedroom may have a single overhead fixture supplying all the ambient light in the room. That's usually not effective for setting a soft and relaxing mood. The best bedroom lighting schemes use several different fixtures with low-wattage bulbs, and many

Nightstand lamps don't necessarily have to match. This cozy bedroom features two different types—an adjustable lamp for the reader in the family, and a more traditional shade lamp for the quick-to-sleep member of the couple.

have no overhead fixture at all. As long as there aren't disconcerting areas of shadow, low light is really more appropriate for this room. Use a combination of lamps so that you control where and how the light is spread throughout the room.

Specific task lighting in the bedroom is limited to a dressing or vanity table where makeup is applied and any work space in the room. A vanity table and mirror are usually best served by diffuse light from fixtures positioned on either side of the mirror. A home office space or small work desk requires a reading lamp with an adjustable head and multiple brightness settings. That said, I personally believe that work spaces should be left out of a primary bedroom whenever possible. It's the opposite message of what the room's furnishings, fixtures, and design are meant to convey.

Closets are the only area in the bedroom where I insist on strong, pervasive light. A good overhead light, helped out by smaller features such as puck lights, is usually the best setup for a reach-in or walk-in closet. You want clothing colors and shapes to read definitively so that you can find them quickly any time you're dressing and can make the right judgments on matching garment with garment.

A Welcoming Guest Bedroom

The strategy for decorating or remodeling a guest bedroom differs from the plan of attack for a primary adult bedroom. Obviously, guests aren't going to need the amount of storage a full-time occupant would, and they aren't going to revel in the personalized touches they would appreciate in their own bedrooms. The dresser can be small, and hanging storage can be limited. Some homeowners even turn the guest bedroom closet into a home office setup. Works for me. I'd just caution you to make the home office area of a guest bedroom concealable and self-contained, so that it doesn't look like you're shuffling your guests off to a spend the night in a work space.

It helps when designing a guest bedroom to think of the hotel experience. The goal is to make overnight guests as comfortable as possible. That should take precedence over making a bold design statement that shows off your decorating prowess. The design of the room should actually be a dialed-back version of the design theme you're using in the rest of the house. Here are some specific guidelines to make guests as comfortable as possible:

Although used as a little girl's room, this is an ideal guest-bedroom design. The Versailles cream and pink colors are certainly appropriate for a girl, but they are also sophisticated and elegant enough to work perfectly in guest quarters. Wall moldings and a modest chandelier reinforce the theme of luxury and style, without cluttering the space. A period-style daybed not only provides incredible visual appeal with its appliquéd moldings, but it also includes a trundle to accommodate more than one sleepover guest.

STORAGE

Where closet space is limited or used for another purpose, you can usually supply all the hanging storage guests will need with a small, freestanding wardrobe or even a wall-mounted shelf with a hanging bar underneath. A small folding stand or bench where guests can put their overnight bag or other luggage is a nice touch.

CLEAR TOP SURFACES

Giving guests room to spread out is key to creating comfort. A place to set down a kit bag, a book, or a purse is a message to a guest that the room is theirs, that they are not just occupying somebody else's room. I decorate guest rooms with a minimum of surface accents. Just lamps, a clock, and maybe a vase for flowers.

LUXURIOUS BEDDING

A guest bedroom is most often used just for sleeping at the end of a busy day. Ensure your guests have a memorable night's sleep by including extra pillows on the bed (they can always toss some off, but it's a bother to get up and ask the host for extra pillows). In my experience, homeowners often try to save money in deco-rating the guest bedroom; the bed is not the place to be thrifty. I suggest buying high-thread-count sheets and a nice natural-fiber blanket or down comforter. A pillow-top mattress pad is a wonderful touch as well and won't break the bank.

NEUTRAL WALL ART

Your family photos on the walls of a guest bedroom remind guests that they are staying in someone else's room. I prefer simple and elegant wall art that reinforces the design style you've set for the room and the house. I also include a mirror in every guest bedroom I decorate, for practical reasons.

LIGHT-BLOCKING WINDOW TREATMENTS

Whether your guests like to sleep in or pop out of bed at the crack of dawn, that's a decision they should make rather than the sun making it for them. Thick, lined drapes also give you the opportunity to add a touch of luxurious texture to the room easily, and really drive home the idea of a sumptuous space that welcomes guests in style.

Thick shades, a comfortable double bed, carpet, and simple furnishings make this guest bedroom a welcome home away from home. The seaside motif is fun but not overdone, and the lack of family photos and personal effects helps the visitor feel like the room is his or her space.

The All-Purpose Kid's Bedroom

A kid's bedroom really isn't just one room. It changes entirely age to age. The design should evolve with the stages in your child's life, which is why I work to make the design of this particular room as adaptable as possible.

A TODDLER'S TEMPORARY DIGS

Let's face it, a baby or toddler's room is more about the look you like than what they prefer. Because this stage passes quickest of all, it's not a great idea to go wild with expensive furnishings or decorative treatments. Usually the furnishings are functional: a crib for sleeping, a changing table, and maybe a rocking chair or other seating. Wall art is usually the most powerful decoration in the room. You can go a bit wild with your color choices because you'll be changing the color scheme in short order. A lot of homeowners like to add stencils or other wall designs; wall decals are an even better choice. You can find a huge selection of decals online, and most are inexpensive. Many of these can be reused, and all are easy to remove when it comes time to redecorate.

The closet and other storage areas are key in the toddler's room. It's wise to set up the closet with modest hanging storage and lots and lots of shelving. Bins and boxes will come in handy for all the odds and ends that go along with tending to a younger child or infant. If there is no closet, or closet space is being used for something else, you might want to look at a shelf-and-bin storage unit for storing everything from baby clothes to picture books in one place. I urge people to buy nicer storage units—such as real wood shelves and wicker baskets—that will still be appropriate for the child as he or she grows.

KID-FRIENDLY GETAWAY

Young children and pre-teens begin to develop a sense of personal space, so it's nice if their room reflects their personality and interests. For instance, let your youngster help you choose the room's colors. A child will often pick shades that might be a little garish, but you can moderate the actual colors you use so that everyone's happy. More important, you should design organization into the room. The biggest challenge parents face, and one of the biggest irritations for parents everywhere, is teaching a child to keep his or her room clean. The right bedroom design will help train children to be orderly. A great technique is to stick pictures on drawer fronts, shelves, and other storage in the room of items

that are supposed to be kept there. If you're a little graphically inclined, you can even make these visual helpers a fun decorative element running throughout the room by drawing your "labels." A kid's closet still needs far more shelving, drawers, and bins than hanging storage. Always include a laundry bag and make it clear what it's used for.

The bed should be comfortable, but it doesn't need to be large. Kids are rambunctious, so any bed in a child's room should be durable. In my experience, the simpler the bed, the better. Basic bunk beds are the right idea for brothers or sisters sharing a room. Bedding is a way to allow the occupant to personalize the space. Let your child choose whatever type of sheets and blankets they want; it won't set you back a lot of money, and it will help give the room an identity your child finds fun and enjoyable. You'll also need storage for toys. The key is variety. Toys come in all different

The young girl who occupies this room is well served by a double bed, with a wealth of storage furniture and a desk for schoolwork. I like to create an area in school-age kids' bedrooms specifically for study—it helps them focus on homework when and where they need to.

Start early with a child's bedroom—while it's still a nursery. A closet organizing system such as this is adaptable and can be reconfigured as the child grows.

sizes and shapes, so the storage needs to accommodate that. I always use open storage for a child's room; the easier it is for a child to get toys in and out of storage, the more likely it is that they will keep their room clean.

TEEN SCENE

I'm a firm believer that teen bedroom design should be driven by the personality of the teen who lives there. Teenagers are just beginning to understand how they want to present and express themselves, and their bedrooms should be sanctuaries to do just that. Be prepared that the design of your teenager's bedroom probably isn't going to follow the aesthetic you've set in the rest of the house. And that's okay.

I set up very specific areas in a teen's room, which are different from the areas you'd define in a younger child's space. Where floor space allows, I add in a casual chair and reading lamp so that the teen can relax with friends and have someplace other than the floor or bed to read, study, or talk on the phone (or all three at once). I also create a study area. It doesn't matter whether you're the parent of an honor student or a less-than-stellar scholar; a study area creates the positive idea of a specific time and place to get work done. Provide plenty of visible, intuitive organization in this area, such as cubby and regular shelving, desktop file folders, and trays. Most teens are not very organized. The more you can figure out their work organization for them, the more you help make them a successful student. You'll find a lot of brightly colored shelves and desktop organizers that can bring flair as well as order to the work/study area. Don't forget to include a comfortable chair; the more comfortable your student is, the more likely he or she will get their studying done.

Teen girls are more prone than boys to participate in developing color schemes and elements such as window treatments. However, that doesn't mean boys don't have a preference. Look to clothing and the wall art your son or daughter chooses for clues about what might be the best colors and graphic style for the space.

A wonderful bedroom playland for a little girl will morph over the years. The furniture can be repainted, or refinished natural, and an underbed play area can be turned into useful storage. Adaptability is key when furnishing a child's bedroom, but as this room plainly shows, that doesn't mean limiting the design.

The measure of success of any bedroom design is how enjoyable and comfortable the room is to live in. It doesn't matter if you've designed the room for yourself, a guest, or a child. If it is a pleasure to the eye *and* leads to great sleep, ease in dressing, and relaxing down time, it's a successful design!

Chapter 4
UNCOMMON COMMON AREAS

The common areas of your home can be divided into two groups: the obvious and not so obvious. Living rooms, family rooms, great rooms, and other spaces dedicated to recreation and socializing are the most apparent common areas. Entryways, foyers, hallways, and staircases are spaces we tend not to notice.

This well-designed living room sets the tone for the whole house, with a beautiful suite of furniture occupying a thoughtful layout centered around the focal-point fireplace. The look is enhanced by a sophisticated color scheme and a wealth of enchanting decorative accents set out on the stage of a nearly ebony African mahogany wood floor.

That doesn't make them less important from a design standpoint though. In fact, these transition spaces are used by almost everyone who enters the house and if they don't command the attention a main room does, they still consistently reinforce your design theme and style.

Design both types of common areas for seamless continuity. Common areas are usually connected to more than one room, so they are the glue that holds your home's interior design together. The living room and family room in particular may set the overall design tone for your home.

Rooms for Living . . . in Style and Comfort

You'll most likely be balancing multiple functions when you design a living room or, to a lesser degree, a family room. The room design must be fluid and make people feel comfortable and at ease as soon as they walk in. But the design also has to establish your sense of style in an up-front way. This is your chance to show off a little!

A separate, independent living room is usually designed to be more formal than other rooms. That doesn't mean the design needs to be stuffy! I don't use fragile pieces of furniture meant to be looked at rather than used, and a good living room design isn't about plastic slipcovers or sterile, "perfect" layouts that invite viewing from a distance rather than living. There's a word for a room like that—it's called a museum. Functionality is huge in my book (one of my big three in fact—practicality). Larger open spaces encompassing both living room and family room, or stand-alone family rooms, are going to be more about pure comfort, relaxation, and enjoying one another's company.

Thoughtfully Place Furniture

The trick in decorating either room is to combine high style with livability. Start with the furniture. Form your living room and family room layouts around "furniture groupings." Never carelessly add a piece of furniture into the room design just because you happen to own a particular table or chair. Like kids in high school, each piece of furniture in a living room or family room has to be part of a specific clique.

Common groupings include the couch–coffee table–easy chair pack and the combo of comfortable chair, reading light, and side

Position common-area furniture in context. The designer of this upscale living room has purposely chosen a symmetrical layout with two curved couches balancing the furniture group, a design that echoes what has been done in the entryway, with matching chairs and accents flanking the entry console table. Always consider furniture placement in relation to views into—and from—other rooms and areas.

table that make up a reading area. Whenever possible, I like to group furniture to take advantage of a distinctive feature such as a fireplace or large picture window. A family room—or a living room that includes the functions of a family room—most likely will also need to accommodate a home theater setup. Whatever the case, group furniture with a purpose in mind.

Once again, turn to your basic floor plan sketch. I like to draw on my room sketches because that's how I've always worked. You may, however, prefer to use furniture cutouts, which is a quick way to try out lots of different room layouts with little fuss or muss. Cutouts work well, especially on larger, open floor plans containing two or three distinct areas.

Whatever tool you're using, the goal is the same: Determine the best overall layout for traffic moving through the room *and* the best position and layout for the furniture in each specific grouping. Keep practical considerations in mind as you work through where the furniture will go. Position seating that will be used during the day so that sunlight streaming through the window will not be in a visitor's eyes. The same holds true for where you place a TV or computer monitor. Make sure you're minimizing glare.

CARTER'S LAW:
Living Room GPS

Free and easy movement is key to comfortable and pleasant living room and family room layouts. The following measurements will help you get there:

- The standard spacing between the front edge of a couch and coffee table is 18 inches. Too far is almost as bad as too close. Don't place the coffee table more than 24 inches from the edge of the sofa.

- Coffee table height will also affect how comfortable the room is. A coffee table should never be higher than the top of the couch cushions and shouldn't be more than 2 or 3 inches lower than that height.

- The distance between seating and a TV screen should ideally be three times the diagonal measurement of the TV's screen. In other words, a 32-inch TV should be positioned 96 inches from a seated person's eyes.

- TV height is a big comfort and viewing issue. The center of the TV screen should be placed in line with a seated person's line of sight as they look straight ahead. Obviously this point is going to vary by a couple of inches up or down depending on how tall the person is. The biggest mistake homeowners make with a home theater setup is positioning the TV way too high.

- The standard buffer zone between seating is 4 to 9 feet. This allows for a sense of intimacy without crowding the area so much that moving around is difficult.

- Leave at least a 24-inch open lane of travel through any living room or family room, although 36 inches is better.

This living room conversation group is perfectly positioned. Notice that there's ample room for navigating both around and through the grouping, yet the pieces are close enough together to maintain a sense of comfortable intimacy.

REPURPOSING WHAT YOU ALREADY HAVE

Laying out your new room design usually entails working with existing furniture. Don't be afraid, though, to swap pieces in and out. We often become attached to certain pieces of furniture, either just because we've had them for so long or because they prompt memories. But if you're going to design a beautiful, useful living room that shows off your taste, you have to be willing to get rid of furniture when the design calls for it.

On the other hand, you can revive many furnishings with just a little bit of work. You don't have to be a former carpenter like me to sand down a wood table and refinish it with a darker or lighter stain, or paint it a fun color.

While we're on the subject of adapting old things to new designs, here's a strong suggestion: Look to salvage before you buy new. It's rare on one of my shows that I don't create a piece of furniture using reclaimed wood, or that we don't restore an existing piece of furniture or a fixture such as an old door in some interesting way to serve a new design. If we can find a piece to salvage and repurpose in someone's home, chances are good that you can find one for your own home. Most of the time, these projects aren't super challenging and just about any homeowner with a basic set of tools and a few hours can pull them off.

The furniture in this colorful space is well balanced—no extremely large or extremely petite pieces to throw off the visual weight of the group. The balance creates a pleasing visual flow that tempers the strength of the vivid green used as the dominant color.

The beauty of repurposing is that it hits the big trifecta of Carter's Way. Repurpose a desk with a new coat of paint or a specialty finish and it becomes part of your customized style. The project is eminently practical because you're saving the cost of a new piece of furniture, and it's totally eco-friendly because you're keeping that desk out of the dump and alleviating the need to harvest materials to replace it. As far as I'm concerned, repurposed furniture is a design home run.

FINDING A BALANCE

New, old, or repurposed, judge all your furnishings on visual weight and balance. It's as easy as this: If the room is noticeably small, use small, detailed, and lightweight furniture. If the room is expansive, feel free to use larger, more substantial pieces. Too many dainty chairs and tables in a large room with high ceilings look a bit off. The same is true of a small living room stuffed to the gills with big roll-arm sofas and gigantic club chairs. When it comes to family rooms, you want to add in the element of cleanability in judging potential furnishings (food and drink have a way of finding their way into comfortable rooms—especially those with a TV).

Maintain balance between furniture in groupings as well. For instance, if you have large, overstuffed, patterned couches and chairs and a tiny glass-topped coffee table, the overall group is going to look off-kilter. Replace the coffee table with a beefier unit to maintain visual balance and appropriate composition.

CARTER'S LAW:
Define with Area Rugs

Help the eye read separate furniture groupings in a room's layout by defining the group with area rugs. While you're at it, take the opportunity to complement upholstery textures and furniture colors with your choice of rug fiber. The various sizes and shapes available mean that one or another will definitely meet the needs of any living room furniture group. However, when you position furniture on the rug, all pieces should either be entirely on the rug or have just the front legs on the rug. Whichever you choose, position all the furniture on the outside of the group in the same way. And don't be a slave to convention; you can even use area rugs on top of carpeting.

The right small area rug can be just as effective in the correct setting as a larger version might be. This rug ties together a handsome living room seating group with stripes that visually link the couch to the chairs. The small size also showcases the spectacular American walnut hardwood floor, adding to the room's look.

So there's your process: Establish the furniture groups you want in the room, position furniture within the groups, and edit pieces in and out as needed to create visual balance, harmony, and an effective room layout.

Finesse your furniture groupings, experimenting with furniture position until the layout completely satisfies you. Get all the main pieces in the right places, and you can move on to the supporting players. In a living room or family room, that usually means adding storage furniture.

A Place for Everything

Begin with a basic storage assessment. That's a fancy way of saying figure out exactly what you need to store and how much (and what type of) space it requires. Actually measure things like books or DVDs, candles, or other items. Once you have a measurement to work with (this is especially important for books and bookshelves) look for the ideal places to put bookshelves, wall-mounted shelves, tables with drawers, or specialized storage. Don't just add end tables or bookshelves for the heck of it; it's never a crime to leave open space in a living room.

Keep in mind that you may be able to double-purpose pieces within your furniture groupings. I love when furniture performs double duty. Shopping for a new coffee table? Consider a trunk as a spacious, great-looking sofa partner with integral storage. Or follow the contemporary trend of using one, two, or three hollow "cubes." I like these increasingly popular options because they're adaptable and come covered in a nice assortment of materials, from leather to stained wood to all kinds of fabrics. Most have a cavity inside for storing small items, and they can be moved

A handsome sideboard adds a simple pattern to a chic living room layout, with plenty of top space and concealed storage hidden behind mirrored doors. Good looking and useful—you can't ask for more from living room storage furniture.

around to suit different layouts. They're also multi-purpose; they can be used in a group as a coffee table or alone as a footstool, end table, or even seating.

Turn to shelves for the most adaptable storage solutions. Look first at those units that will accommodate everything you need to store (with a 10- to 15-percent buffer for error and growth). Then pick a style that fits your decor. Floating shelves—in which the mounting hardware is concealed—are popular for just about any design theme, although they aren't recommended for heavy objects. Freestanding shelf units are going to be the option of choice for keeping a large number of disparate objects in order. Complete units with shelves and slide-out fabric bins or wicker baskets can be informally chic and perfect for toys, games, or other entertainment odds and ends in a family room. A backless bookshelf can serve as a room divider or even a display piece for a collection of statuettes or other art.

Complete the room's layout before moving on to lighting, decorating, or any other stage. The right furnishings in the right places are the bones of your design. Make sure your room has a solid skeleton before you add the other elements.

Built-in shelves can be both a design focal point and accessible storage in a living room or family room. If you're willing to go to the trouble and expense of a built-in unit such as this, include both cabinets and shelves for ultimate flexibility. You can also find prefab units designed to look like built-ins.

Carter's Case Study:
The Bluestein Family Room

As a busy couple and devoted parents, David and Allison Bluestein's free time was pretty much consumed by work, community activities, or family time. That didn't leave much of a chance to tackle the challenges of redesigning an overworked and undersized living room. Even though it functioned as the social center of the house, the room was a cramped, uncomfortable, poorly designed space. The oversized TV sat squarely in front of the fireplace, rendering what could have been a hallmark feature useless, and the couple couldn't move through the room without literally tripping over each other or the family's three dogs. As David put it, "We're constantly walking into things; even the dogs walk into things." On top of everything else, the heavy traffic had given the room a well-worn look.

It was obviously time to redo things Carter's Way.

We started as we almost always do by clearing out the room and making a few crucial decisions in discussions with the homeowners. David and Allison wanted a "rustic, Spanish style" design that was thoroughly comfy and warm. It had to be a place where they could hunker down and enjoy their time with their son, as well as entertain on a regular basis.

The first order of business was to turn the hidden fireplace into the showcase feature it deserved to be. I roped in Allison as my helper, and we started

A cramped layout masked the decorative potential in the Bluesteins' living room–family room combo.

The TV blocked a potentially dynamite fireplace.

working on a pine frame. I wanted to clad the fireplace column in copper sheeting to increase the light and add color in a room that was probably going to be a little light-challenged (Spanish and rustic themes are inevitably full of dark colors and light-absorbing textures). Copper is a great look for these sorts of themes, and the metal ages beautifully. To give the feature a little something extra, I decided to trim it out in reclaimed boards for a truly old-world look.

Allison and I built the pine frame pretty quickly. It was just a matter of some careful measurements and screwing pine 2 x 4s together following a quick sketch. Pine is ideal for simple sub-structures like this because it's easy to work with and inexpensive. The next step was to distress the copper sheet to give it an aged feel. I put together a crude wood mallet and embedded several round-headed rivets in the face to make a distressing tool.

Metal sheets of any sort are wonderful decorative touches, and most are easy to cut and shape to whatever purpose you have in mind. You can alter the appearance as we did by pounding the surface with a texturing tool or by using other instruments to mark the surface in different ways. The many metals available in sheet

CARTER'S WAY

form offer lots and lots of potential looks. You'll find large sheets at most home centers.

Once we had textured the copper, we attached it to the pine frame with copper nails. A little hammering on the edges to wrap them around the frame's outline, and the entire unit was ready for mounting.

While we formed the copper, designer Jinnie Choi was hard at work painting the walls a light parchment tan. The neutral color would provide the perfect backdrop to the wood tones and dark-colored accents that inevitably play a role in a Spanish-style design theme. She also helped us prepare the fireplace by refinishing the white-painted hearth in a more natural dark stone color and texture. Then she finished the walls by painting two arched rectangles on either side of where the TV would sit. The rectangles would be the backgrounds for two arched shelf units carpenter Jake Scott was building. Jinnie painted the area that would show through the shelves using a turquoise base with copper-colored stippling. The turquoise matched what she was going to use on a decorative accent over the front door. Using accent colors repetitively like this is a perfect way to unify a room's design.

The finished fireplace serves as a spectacular focal point for the room, and the copper cladding adds color, texture, and brightness.

Jake wasn't standing around while all this work was going on; he was busy cutting the legs for two new tables we were adding to the room. First came the table on which the TV would sit. We had decided to use a salvaged dark wood door as the tabletop. Jake cut legs from new 4 x 4s. He matched the time-worn finish of the door by scorching the newer lumber with a torch and scrubbing the surface with a wire brush. The result was a surface that looked all of a piece with the much older door.

Jake built a matching console table to position behind the sofa using reclaimed planks that he fastened together with biscuit dowels and glue. He stained the planks and attached 4 x 4 legs with the same aged appearance he had used on the TV table.

After finishing the tables, Jake helped me mount the framed copper cladding onto the existing brick column by drilling masonry screws through the wood frame and into the mortar joints between bricks. We finished the fireplace by trimming the column with thick reclaimed wood planks screwed together into ceiling-to-hearth corner trim pieces. We attached the lumber running up either side of the fireplace, creating the illusion of aged supporting posts.

The copper column looked tremendous in place. It was the ideal focal point that we had all envisioned to start with, but we still had a lot of work left. Jake started in on the two arched shelf display units that would hold decorative plates and be mounted on the wall on either side of the TV. Arched shapes are common to Spanish and rustic design styles. Stained dark, they would be right at home with all the other furniture.

I had a bigger challenge to deal with. The existing paneled cathedral ceiling was a great look for a country or contemporary design theme, but it wasn't going to work so well with the design style we were after. Added to that, tar from the roof had leaked down through the paneling in drips that marred the sides of the exposed joists. The solution was to enclose the ceiling with eco-friendly cherry veneer tongue-in-groove paneling.

The paneling is manufactured with more than 90 percent recycled materials. Just as important, the mid-range red tone perfectly satisfied Allison's desire for a warm and cozy look in the space. I installed the boards just as you would a tongue-in-groove floor, but on the ceiling. This covered the joists but left the central header beam exposed. I stained the beam a couple shades darker than the cherry for a more dramatic look and used $3/4$-inch cove molding pin-nailed around the edges of the ceiling for a truly finished look.

The reclaimed door accent introduces an incredible decorative element, especially with the backlit faux stained-glass panel. Always look for accent opportunities like this.

The big parts of the room were complete. All that remained was a special accent feature that Jinnie had been working on. She had picked up a door at the same salvage yard where we found the door for the TV table. After removing a central panel in the door, she repainted the remaining wood framework a distressed turquoise. She then measured and cut a piece of glass perfectly sized to fit into the opening. Using some antique moldings as stencils, she painted the glass with Stained Glass Paint. Real stained glass is colored through and through as part of the manufacturing process. But where nobody will touch the glass, you can use this paint to create a similar effect on an accent window. The paint adheres to glass or acrylic and is translucent so that it looks just like real stained glass. It comes in a rainbow of jewel-toned colors.

After the glass dried, Jinnie installed the panel in the door opening and we hung the door sideways in front of an open soffit at the front-door end of the ceiling. The soffit was already wired with soffit lights, which made the faux stained glass sparkle and added a crowning accent to the room.

Jake replaced the underpowered overhead fan lighting fixture with fairly inconspicuous track lighting fixtures that blended right into the ceiling. The track lights can be adjusted to throw light exactly where it's needed. That was a big upgrade over the room's existing lighting.

All that remained was to arrange the furnishings and add some theme-appropriate accents. The new design accommodated both the TV and the now-jaw-dropping fireplace. The new tables and wall-mounted shelves helped establish the theme and made for a more comfortable and usable space.

We replaced a fan-light fixture with these adjustable track lights. The fixtures themselves are modest, but they cast a nice light and, more important, the light can be directed all around the room simply by moving the track heads.

The All-Encompassing Entertainment Center

Design a living room or family room these days, and chances are pretty good that one space you need to plan—"plan" being the operative word—is a home theater of one sort or another. This can be the sole focus of a family room or it can be a substantial area of a larger, more general-purpose room. Either way, it's a unique area that begs to be properly designed.

Designing a home entertainment center into a family room—or a larger living room or great room—is about creating an enjoyable experience while ensuring that home electronics and related media don't overwhelm the room's design. Given today's diversity of audio, video, and gaming equipment, it's no wonder that keeping an entertainment center contained is one of the biggest home-design challenges.

Furniture manufacturers have responded to this technological proliferation. You can find an entertainment center, or the pieces to make one, that matches exactly the size, shape, and mix of your home entertainment components.

Take the opportunity of choosing an entertainment center to solve storage needs as well. A unit like this, with a wealth of open shelving, can not only position TV and all your media in a logical and viewer-sensitive way, it also adds abundant space for books or decorative accents—a dual-purpose slam dunk!

Sometimes modest is better. This glass-front media cabinet provides all the storage necessary for a basic home theater setup. A larger unit would have been a space hog, and an unnecessary addition to this small family room.

DEEP GREEN CHOICES: Curbing Thirsty Electronics

By some estimates, home electronics use up to 70 percent of their electricity in standby mode. This means you pay a pretty penny for electricity that's doing nothing other than keeping the clocks inside TVs, stereos, DVD players, and other electronics running nonstop, or maintaining a warm-up mode. Save money and the planet by putting your home electronics on a plug strip with a switch. When they aren't being used, cut off the juice and watch the savings pile up.

But before you run out and buy a pre-made monster entertainment center, give the same amount of thought to your home theater and electronics setup as you did to your storage. Ask yourself a few relevant questions. Do you really need all your DVDs or CDs? Maybe it's time to give up those Van Halen tapes, or consolidate. Chances are, you may have songs or movies in electronic format, or subscribe to a service that does, in which case it might be wise to give away or donate some of your media. Are

CARTER'S LAW:
Keep Cables under Control

Cables snaking down walls, across shelves, or hanging under tables are just plain ugly, and they undermine your well-thought-out design. There's no excuse for letting cables harsh your design style, because there are scads of cable organizers available in home improvement catalogs and through many large retailers. You'll find cable cords that wrap up a group of cables in one neat, flexible housing; cable conduit that can be painted to completely conceal cables; and an assortment of screw-on or clip-on cable brackets for shelves, tabletops, and other surfaces. Choose the organizers that work best with your electronics storage and furniture, and keep wires and cables out of sight where they belong.

Large, all-in-one wall units such as this one often include concealed cable runs, and the sheer size of the piece covers up the wall outlet in any case, hiding power cables. This entertainment center is a wonderful addition to an eclectic family room, but snaking cables and wires would have diminished that look.

you planning on upgrading your electronics soon? If you are, a room redesign may be the perfect opportunity to buy a new TV or stereo. Replacing a traditional CRT TV (the type with the big, bulging backside) with a flat-panel TV opens up possibilities and may reduce your furniture needs. You can mount a flat-panel TV right on the wall, for instance, or place it on a much more modest table or shelf. In addition, stereo or home-theater components continue to be miniaturized, and more and more are wireless (such as surround-sound speakers), so that a new setup may take far less room than your existing entertainment system does.

That means that the first step to getting your entertainment area in order is shedding, replacing, or buying whatever electronics you had planned on acquiring.

Only when you're sure exactly what gear will form the heart of your home theater or audio setup can you effectively position the furniture you'll need to keep everything in order and make the most of your viewing and listening experience. Buy or repurpose a complete home entertainment center if that works best for you. These are good all-in-one solutions—choose based on the storage and features you need (concealed storage, shelving, special cable runways).

However, keeping in mind that one of the three key parts of Carter's Way is customized style, you might want to personalize how you store and present your electronics. It's pretty easy to repurpose a small table, an old door, or simple shelves (or a combination) to serve as home for your video and audio equipment. Bring your own touch to a home entertainment center and you may wind up not only creating a dynamite focal point for the room but also enhancing your viewing and listening pleasure as well.

Making the Most of Transition Spaces

It's easy to forget about the decorative style of transition spaces throughout the house. Entry halls, mudrooms, hallways, and staircases are all places we spend a lot of time going through but don't usually notice. Well, it's time to pay some attention.

These types of areas either set the tone for rooms in the house or help maintain a design style already established. That means your goal for these spaces is twofold: make them look like they fit with the rest of the house, and make them attractive and welcoming in their own right.

Threshold areas, including entry halls, formal foyers, and rough-and-tumble mudrooms, are all chances to send a message to anyone entering your house. Let's start at the front.

Make your entryway welcoming by keeping it sparsely furnished and simple. I rarely see the need for significant furnishings beyond the traditional trio of wall-mounted mirror, console table, and entryway seating. Use an entryway mirror to add a decorative

flourish in the form of the shape and frame you choose. Go with a rectangle or square if your design is leaning toward a formal or more reserved look; pick an oval or round mirror to suit a more casual decor.

Select a table in a style that complements the rest of the design, fits perfectly in the available space, and has ample top surface for things like mail, packages, and a bowl or basket to keep car keys and cell phones in one place. Because an entryway table is one of only a couple pieces of furniture in the space, it can be fairly distinctive. Here's a chance for you to be creative and use a table you've repainted or refinished just for the space. I've even seen homeowners repurpose small dressers for this purpose. Just keep in mind that whatever table you use needs to work with the available space and your chosen design style.

Seating is essential in an entryway, as far as I'm concerned. It provides a place for people to wait for others, put on shoes or boots, or wrestle children into their cold-weather gear. A single

Minimal furnishings and elegant flooring make this an attractive entryway and perfect transition area.

chair usually won't cut it; I'd advise you to add bench seating of some sort to your entryway. A plain backless bench is fine for a smaller space, although you can choose one to reinforce a more ornate style or larger foyer as well.

If your entryway sees a lot of traffic, the space might be well served by a freestanding or wall-mounted coat rack. Again, choose one that takes up as little space as possible, while still accommodating the maximum number of coats you expect to hang. Coat hooks are often the best solution that lets you place informal hanging storage exactly where you need it. Hooks are also a chance to add small accents to an entry space.

A mudroom is a slightly different case. Outfit this informal space with more storage and more durable furniture—especially pieces featuring integral storage. The single biggest detractor to

Given the various things that are stored in a mudroom, it makes sense to buy an all-in-one unit like this one with hanging, hidden, and shelf storage, so that with one piece of furniture you have a place for everything.

CARTER'S WAY

a mudroom's look is clutter in the form of loose sports equipment, outerwear, and other odds and ends. Bench seats with space underneath for shoes or sporting gear, cubby shelves, hanging hooks, and large all-in-one mudroom units incorporating both concealed and exposed storage can all serve you well in a busy back or side-door entrance space. The key is to add usable pieces that store and provide seating but are sized and shaped correctly to allow traffic to flow freely through the space and into the house.

The mudroom is one case where I think you can find so many great, inexpensive all-in-one solutions on the market that you don't need to struggle to come up with the perfect arrangement of benches, hooks, cabinets, and shelves. Someone's already done all the thinking for you, and you'll find complete mudroom solutions in styles from sleek and modern to tough and traditional. If you have more than one child (plus friends and pets) who uses an entrance other than the front door, one of these solutions is for you.

Regardless of the furniture you use, the rule in the mudroom is to organize in style. Create a place for everything that might be stored in the room to stop people from tripping over umbrellas or creating an unsightly pile of galoshes and hiking boots. In my house in Michigan, I have a basket that holds hats and gloves for the winter. Not only does it organize the clutter, but I simply put away the whole basket in the summer. Keep the room looking organized and you keep the mess out of the rest of the house and establish a streamlined attractive look for this transition space.

Common-Area Color Schemes

You have a lot more latitude in developing a color scheme for a living room or family room than you will in an entry hall, hallway, or staircase. Common living areas are usually some of the larger rooms in a house, and they provide you with a lot of actual surface area across which to coordinate different colors. Transition spaces are usually much smaller and not as naturally well lit.

The larger living areas entail more options and therefore more consideration. Develop a color scheme based on the activities that will take place in a living room and family room, as well as the feeling you want to establish in the room.

- Establish a calm, low-key, harmonious look in a living room with lighter, cooler colors arranged in an analogous or monochromatic color scheme.

- Give any living room used for abundant entertaining a high-energy charge with a warm color scheme. If the room is large, take some risks; use strong colors in a complex color scheme such as triadic or complementary. Add white, gray, or neutral to create negative areas that separate the colors and give the eye restful pauses between splashes of vibrant color. If the room is smaller or oddly shaped, stick to a monochromatic or analogous color scheme, or rely on neutral colors.

- Add energy to more subtle living room designs with bursts of bright or bold color used as accent colors in a largely neutral color scheme.

- Enrich a home theater with darker warm, cool, or neutral colors. A neutral color scheme will provide an especially supportive background to movies or sports seen on a large-screen TV. Create more or less visual interest in a neutral scheme by how much you vary the colors used. Range from sand to dark chocolate, for instance, for a vibrant backdrop to your multimedia space.

- Go sophisticated in a formal, elegant living room with a combination of grays and black and white accents. Add patterns in upholstery and window treatments to make the look subtle but stunning.

The designer of this understated beige living room added a surprisingly bold gold as the accent color. Unexpected and beautiful, the color brings richness and energy to the room, and the color scheme is kept in balance by the larger areas of neutral colors.

This cozy living room uses a low-key analogous color scheme, but it adds lots of excitement with a stunning mix of patterns and textures. The combination of patterns is just right, balanced with lots of "negative space" between them so the patterns aren't fighting each other.

- Brighten and warm up a basement family room with unexpectedly rich and bright warm colors, such as tangerine, canary yellow, and accents of fire-engine red.

Transition spaces are a somewhat different case. Because they are so modest in size, they are usually colored with only one or at most two hues. Entryway colors, however, must work harder than those in any other transition space. The colors must create a welcoming environment while making a design statement of their own. That statement has to be tempered by the need to give cues about the rooms beyond the entryway. That's a lot for a color or colors to do.

Use any type of color scheme to achieve these goals, but the easiest to implement are going to be analogous, monochromatic, and neutral schemes—the safest and most common choices. In fact, you can tap a popular designer technique and color the entryway and hallways throughout the house the same neutral color.

Hallways are often best colored in neutrals or lighter tones that increase the sense of space. Distinctive cherry wood flooring and a singular focal point sculpture save this particular beige-toned hallway from boredom.

Where the entryway is self-contained—such as a formal foyer—you have more latitude in what you do with color. Because entryways should be sparsely furnished, I'd suggest you stick with a two-color scheme. There's simply not a lot of room or need for spicing up the design with strong accent colors. However, many entryways are open to other rooms or hallways leading to rooms. Tie the entryway to other spaces by using a single color from the color scheme used in connecting rooms, or by using shades or tints of those colors.

Mudrooms call for more robust colors. You can still tie the mudroom to the room it lets into, but I'd recommend going a shade or two darker and using warm colors—they're welcoming and they don't show dirt as readily as light colors do.

Hallways and staircases are, of course, special cases. They aren't actual rooms, but they still need to be decorated and thoughtfully colored. Although I rarely add furniture to a hallway, I believe the colors should be well thought out. Don't just paint the hallway white and call it a day. You can be much more imaginative than that.

Steer clear of patterns in hallways because the spaces are easily overwhelmed. That doesn't mean you should allow your hallways to be boring. The modest wall surfaces are ideal for special effects such as a rag rolling or sponging, and pale versions of bolder or darker colors used in the connecting rooms will usually serve the spaces well.

Staircases, especially those just off an entryway, are often best served by a very light, neutral color. The off-white in this passageway is a perfect example. The sedate color allows for the incredible architectural detailing to grab the eye without competition.

Shedding Light on Common Areas

Lighting is where differences between common areas become most apparent. Your lighting plan for a formal living room will be appreciably different from your plan for a family room, which will be entirely different than lighting in hallways or entryways.

Living room lighting is often the most complex to work out of any room in the house, other than the kitchen. Start by establishing the general ambient light sources. You'll most often look to an overhead fixture to serve as the central source of dispersed light, adding "fill" lighting by strategically placing floor and table lamps. The whole goal of ambient light is to eliminate disconcerting shadows and provide pleasing illumination throughout the room, maintaining a modest contrast between light and dark areas. Make the room too dark and it will seem unwelcoming and foreboding; too light and it will look like a hospital waiting room.

Your furniture groupings are now in place, so you'll already have specific surfaces available for table lamps. Position these first to get an idea of how well the light from those fixtures penetrates into the space. Then add floor lamps as needed to round out the general lighting in the room. Balance floor lamp positioning to get the right light in the right place without interrupting the layout or traffic flow through the room. Move fixtures around until you achieve a pleasing level of dispersed lighting throughout the room. Then move on to task lighting.

Task lighting in living rooms and family rooms most commonly takes the form of reading lights. You'll find these handy additions alongside couches and, of course, partnered with easy chairs to create a specific reading area.

You can make dramatic design statements with the common area lighting fixtures you choose. Here, a powerful chandelier provides excellent ambient lighting, while sconces on either side of the fireplace add fill lighting and a reading light next to the sofa serves as task lighting.

Similar to task lighting is the need to effectively light a TV or home theater. Few people truly understand how lighting actually affects TV viewing. A TV in a completely dark room can lead to eye strain. If the room is brightly lit, the colors are not as vivid as they should be. The best viewing situation is a small amount of light shining behind the TV panel if possible. This modest glow will help your eyes adjust smoothly between areas of bright and dark and will help the image on the screen come forward. Ideally soft lights should be projected on either side behind the TV.

Finish off your living room or family room lighting with accent lights. These can be specialized fixtures that light art on walls, hidden cove fixtures that dramatically uplight the ceiling, and shelf lights on bookshelves. I limit the accent lights I use in a room because I think they can easily be overused, but they can be effective in certain areas where the general illumination is not penetrating.

Keep in mind that the light any fixture emits will be affected by the lampshade. Correct lampshade size is essential because you should never position a bare bulb in direct line of sight. The more light you want the fixture to supply, the more sheer the shade should be. Different colored shades can tint light; yellow shades will give light a yellow cast that flatters skin tones but makes details in the space indistinct. White shades will usually cast a bluer, brighter light. Try testing out a few different lampshades to find the one that creates the best ambiance and looks right with your room design.

Your options for lighting entryways, hallways, and staircases are going to be somewhat limited. The first concern in these areas is lighting for safety.

- Entryways should have at least two distinct light sources. Most entry halls and foyers have an overhead light that is usually brighter than most other room light sources in the house because the need to see clearly in this space and the fact that people spend a limited amount of time there mean that pure illumination is more important than a soft, diffused light. Add

Stair-step lighting is a practical matter in transition areas, especially where the stairs aren't directly lit. Under-step lighting in an open-riser system such as the stairs shown here is especially effective to protect against stumbles and falls.

A chandelier provides great lighting for an entryway, especially one with warm hues and dark hardwood flooring. The overhead light is helped by sconces and bleed-over illumination from adjacent areas.

a table lamp to the entryway table specifically to illuminate small items such as keys and cell phones so that they can be quickly located on the way out of the house. When positioning a table lamp or other secondary lighting source in an entryway, be careful to avoid hot spots—direct reflections of strong light sources—in the entryway mirror. When you're hanging a mirror, always check that it doesn't reflect a lightbulb or strong overhead fixture back into a person's eyes.

• Mudrooms also require bright lighting for many of the same reasons. Accent lights illuminating cubby storage, cabinets, and even bench cavities are great additions to this room.

- Hallway lighting is a much more limited affair. In most cases, you'll use the lighting that already exists in the space. If the space is wide enough or opens on an alcove, a table lamp may supplement the lighting, but basic is usually best in hallways.

- Staircases are usually well lit by surrounding rooms and areas. However, many staircases are equipped with overhead lights, and those with relatively high ceilings or open landings are your chance to exercise a bit of flair. Use a chandelier or stylish hanging pendants to add color, form, and pattern to what are normally fairly understated passageways.

Work Areas

Most of us don't have the luxury of dedicating an entire room in the house to a home office. Even if you do, most home offices just don't need that much space. More often than not, home work spaces—whether they're used simply to balance the checkbook and answer mail, or for a full-time job—are integrated into other rooms. Living rooms and family rooms are perhaps the most common sites for home offices. That said, the techniques for integrating a home office into a larger room can be used whether you're adding it in a corner of the living room or off to the side of a larger bedroom.

Always blend the work space into the larger room. The easiest way to do this is by matching materials. A desk of the same wood and finish as console and end tables in the living room will visually make the desk part of the living room suite. You can choose a desk that matches the look and material of corner bookshelves where the desk is placed. Use the same principle with other decorative elements: Match the work light you use in your home office to the other fixtures in the room, and select desktop elements such as pen holders, boxes, and bins to match other accents in the room.

Area rugs work as well for defining a home office area as they do for delineating larger furniture groupings. The carpet tiles used here add both color and texture, and perfectly complement the contemporary desk and the white shelves behind.

Integrate a home office by choosing a desk and furnishings that work with the rest of the room. This detailed wood desk perfectly complements the flagstone fireplace.

Whenever you integrate a heavy-use work space like this into a common area—living room, hall, or family room—protect the existing flooring with a chair mat. Make a statement by choosing a mat in a distinctive material such as the bamboo shown here.

Treat the office itself as a miniature furniture grouping. Use an area rug to define the work space as an independent area and to separate it from other parts of a living room or family room. Design the storage as you would in other areas, such as a home theater. Don't just leave papers and work materials lying on shelves; use bins, boxes, and other custom containers to exploit their decorative potential, keep your work space organized, and make the home office look like just another discreet area of the room.

In smaller living rooms, or where you don't want to call attention to the work space, look for convertible furnishings. This "pivot" table can be stowed so that, with the chair tucked in, it takes up the minimal visual space of a console table.

Endless Accenting

Accenting a living room, family room, or other common area is your way of putting your own stamp and style on the design theme you've selected. Unlike a bedroom, where the accents should mean something to you, common area accents should be unique and should move the overall design forward. The right accents will make a good room great.

Think of accents as evolving decorative features. Changing your accents over time is a fantastic way of quickly freshening up the space and making it appear new to people who visit often.

This elegant living room design includes tasteful accents that stop just short of being clutter. A side-table vase mimics the color and shape of the lamp, creating visual balance, and small sculptures personalize the space. I especially like the innovative approach to the soft ottoman as coffee table—by topping it with a tray, the homeowner added a solid stable surface to hold decorative accents and the occasional bottle of wine.

WALL DECORATION

Start accessorizing your space with wall-hung art and photos. The way you display these decorations separates a thoughtful and high-quality decor from a more amateurish and less satisfying result. The biggest mistake homeowners I work with make in decorating their walls is to hang every piece of art or every framed photo they own. The truth is, if you want to effectively show off photos or art to their best advantage, you need to be picky about

CARTER'S LAW:
Hang Art to Be Seen

Hanging art and photos is equal parts math and graphic art. How you position them in the space and in a grid (or a more random pattern) is the art. The science is ideal viewing height. (Keep in mind that you may need to bend or even break these rules to accommodate your particular space. The goal is always to create the most attractive room.)

- The center of a photo or piece of art should be positioned 60 to 62 inches up from the floor (homeowners usually hang art and photos too high). This creates an ideal viewing perspective for people of different heights. Obviously, if you're using a stacked grid, the optimal height will be different. If you're stacking an odd number of rows, hang them so the center of the center row is about 60 inches above floor level. If you're hanging even numbers of rows, divide them in half and hang them so that the tops of the frames on the bottom half of the grid hang at 60 inches.

- A wall-hung piece should not be wider than three-quarters of the width of a piece of furniture underneath it.

- Whether hanging photos in a uniform grid or a more random pattern, leave the exact same amount of space between photos to create visual continuity.

A six-picture grid centered behind this sofa is hung so that the top row is at ideal eye level—a concession to the sloping ceiling. The single piece of artwork next to the glass doors is hung lower than normal because it will most regularly be viewed by people seated on the couch. Always consider viewing perspective when hanging art.

what you put up on your walls. Think about how professional galleries and museums display art and photos. They don't fill the walls with every piece they have at their disposal. Instead, they carefully choose pieces that work together and place them where they will show most effectively. You have to be equally as selective.

Whether you're hanging multiple pieces of art or a single photo, sample the positioning. Do this by cutting out a large piece of paper or posterboard in the same size and shape as the art or photo. Put it in position and view it from several points in the room. This is a great way to lay out a number of pieces that will hang together. It allows you to play with positioning and quickly change things so you can find the optimal arrangement of wall-hung decorations.

CANDLES

Lit or not, candles provide wonderful decorative accents in any room, but especially common areas. Longer, thinner tapers create a formal and elegant look. Shorter, squat pillar candles suggest

A trio of wood textured pillar candles on a side table and a white pillar candle in a wrought iron candle stand next to the fireplace add lovely changeable accents that look nice whether they're lit or not.

a more casual style that can work in any room. Votive candles provide a subtle touch that looks great in any decor style, indoors or out.

Taper candles are necessarily paired with candleholders, which provide as much decorative potential as the candles themselves. When choosing candleholders and candles, keep in mind that candles of different heights create more visual interest than those that are all a single height. Although tapers come in many different colors, the most classic and sophisticated are white or yellow. Tapers are usually used in groups of two or three, or in candelabras. Choose holders based on the material and look that best fit into your design. Simple silver holders complement a wide range of styles, as do glass. Crystal holders are a more formal look, while pewter is a more casual style.

Pillars are some of the most common and popular styles for their design adaptability—they simply look good just about anywhere. Create an eye-catching collection of pillars using different heights and diameters. Although most pillars are dripless, gather a pillar grouping on a platter or other protective surface to catch wax in the event of an overflow. Colored pillars are available, but the vast majority are yellow.

Sprinkle votive candles around like stars in the sky. You can group them as you would pillars or tapers, but because they are all the same height, the most effective decorative use of votives is as repetitive elements on shelves or tabletops. Votive holders are often spectacularly beautiful, in materials such as blown glass. Placed around the room they are subtle color and light accents.

**CARTER'S LAW:
Decorate Oddly**

The eye is most intrigued by groupings of odd numbers of objects. You can add visual interest in your design—and especially when accenting a room—by using three, five, or any other odd number of decorative elements in a group.

This room design is well served by a few simple accents including decorative woven wood balls, a white orchid in a lacquered pot, and a wood bowl full of apples.

TEXTILES

Add texture and color to your room design with fabric accents. Among the most popular and most effective are throw pillows. Position these on couches, chairs, or even daybeds (bolsters and other decorative pillows are traditional accents for standard beds). You'll find throw pillows in just about every fabric imaginable and in patterns and solids subtle to bold. Pick a fabric that creates variation in the design—usually a contrasting fabric to the couch and chairs—and a pattern or color that complements

A beautiful, dark-stained birch hardwood floor sets the stage for this well-accented living room. Coffee table sculptures add form and texture, the potted plant provides contrast and a pleasing irregular shape, and the pictures dress up the wall.

the room's color scheme. A floor cushion is a type of throw pillow that serves as informal seating and large decorative accent. Choose a shape that suits the other lines in the space and a size that fits the available area.

BOWLS AND VASES

Dress up tabletop surfaces and decorative shelves with bowls, vases, and similar vessels. These are usually all about form. Combine different shapes and materials for an interesting mix or use a single material such as blown glass in a number of different forms. Use the same logic you would with other decorative elements. Colors should complement the color scheme. Geometric forms are usually a more formal and staid look, while flowing organic shapes are more casual and artistic.

SCULPTURE, ARTIFACTS, AND COLLECTIONS

It's easy to overdecorate with small art pieces and especially collectibles. Just as you did with your wall-hung art, edit decorative tabletop pieces and collections. Any time you're working with more than one figure, look for a pleasing composition. The easiest is large to small from back to front. Collections need to be given the room they deserve; if you don't have the proper space to display a collection, either edit down the collection, or find a larger space. You also need to be very critical of what's worth showing and what's not. A good way to discern is absolute value. Would someone pay to buy the collection? If not, you probably don't want to use the collection as a decorative element.

A little decorative flair in the form of accents is the icing on the cake of your common-area design. Balance establishing your personality in the space against pure aesthetics and you're sure to wind up with common areas that exhibit a unique and well-developed style.

Chapter 5
PERSONALIZED PRIVATE LUXURY

The bathroom is the most intimate room in the house. Thoughtful bathroom design focuses on making function elegant, and making the daily necessities of life and personal hygiene easier and more enjoyable. The best bathroom designs actually elevate the functional aspect to something akin to a spa-like experience. At the very least, the room should be pleasant, perfectly lit, and super efficient.

It's not hard to design a bathroom well. It's simply a matter of keeping in mind a few key essentials. The space has to be lit for maximum safety and comfort. All the surfaces must be easy to clean because hygiene is the most important consideration in any bathroom, and general grime is the surest way to kill a bathroom design. The room should include luxuries wherever possible, and accents play a big role in what is often the smallest room in the house.

I always begin planning a bathroom design by considering the "spotlight" feature or features I want the space to include. A spotlight can be a special surface material such as a marble tile floor or a glass tile shower stall, it can be a showcase vanity countertop or the addition of his-and-hers sinks, or it can even be a brand new feature such as

A tiled shower stall and a large tub spell luxury in this medium-sized bathroom. The choice of green as the dominant color gives the room a relaxing vibe, one that is reinforced by the use of natural materials throughout.

a whirlpool tub or a stand-alone shower enclosure. A complete bathroom remodel may even include more than one design spotlight. The special feature or features you choose to include in your design will ultimately depend in large part on what type and size of bathroom you're designing.

The Three Levels of Home Bathrooms

There are three basic types of bathrooms, primarily based on size. Each calls for a different decorating and design strategy to make the best use of available space and to accommodate the specific people who will use the room the most. Each presents its own challenges and opportunities.

Bring your half-bath to life with stunning surfaces like the materials included in this showcase bathroom. A soapstone counter and a wall of stone tiles complement the wood vanity and tile floor. Every surface begs to be touched.

THE POWDER ROOM

Sometimes called a half-bath, this is a secondary bathroom mostly used by guests and not directly linked to any given bedroom. The powder room sees limited use, mostly for people to wash their hands or use the toilet. There is no bathtub or shower enclosure. Because this type of bathroom is usually located close to the common areas of the home, it's often decorated to match the color schemes, patterns, and accents in the living room, kitchen, family room, or dining room. Powder rooms are actually great spaces in which to make stunning design statements. You're not dealing with the kind of moisture you would in other bathrooms, so the range of materials you can use in a powder room is naturally greater. Coupled with the small surface area of the floors and walls, this means you can use high-end wallpaper, marble tiles, one-of-a-kind sinks, or other high-end features without breaking your budget.

DETACHED BATH OR GUEST BATH

This is the traditional bathroom used by guests and family near the sleeping quarters. The bathroom is usually located off a hall shared with bedrooms, and most commonly includes a tub with a shower, a single sink and vanity, and an operable medicine chest. There is enough space in this type of room to elaborate a well-thought-out design, but room for luxury elements is usually limited. There may or may not be space enough for a separate shower enclosure, a large spa tub, or his-and-hers sinks. These bathrooms are also sometimes "Jack and Jill" setups, connecting two rooms and equipped with doors to both. That can complicate how you decorate the room.

Even in relatively modest space, a detached bathroom can include a lot of attractive features. The separate shower enclosure hides a steam setup and the extra-deep tub offers a soaking experience for guests or family.

MASTER BATH

A master bath is normally part of a suite with the master bedroom. It serves only that bedroom—the only door leads to the bedroom. Larger, newer homes may feature the equivalent of a master bath positioned as a common bathroom serving other bedrooms. In any case, the master bathroom is usually the largest and most opulent in the house. The room often features a separate tub and shower enclosure, an enclosed water closet (toilet area), double sinks, vanities and mirrors, and occasionally a bidet. The fixtures are often high-end versions, such as a multihead or steam shower, multijet tub, and toilet with seat warmers. A well-designed master bath can convincingly replicate a spa experience in your home.

A stunning "neo" enclosure such as this one can be purchased as a pre-fab unit. But as this shower shows, even a pre-fab unit can look totally fab.

Carter's Case Study:
The Garrett Bathroom

The first time I walked into Steve and Sam Garrett's bathroom, I immediately noticed something was missing. Something big: no shower and no tub, and a big empty space where they might have been.

The couple had spent the four years after they bought the house renovating every room including a downstairs bathroom. The downstairs bathroom had been the biggest challenge, one that had tested their patience and their marriage. They just didn't have it in them to go the whole route again with the master bath. They managed to tear out an old dingy bath and shower and to put up some paint and wainscoting to hide the less-than-perfect wall surfaces, but that was it. A carpet remnant covered an unfinished floor. There was clearly a need for some Carter's Way magic to bring the bathroom together without tearing Steve and Sam apart.

The bathroom was large with lots of potential, and the Garretts had some definitive ideas to launch the design direction. First off, they wanted a tub *and* a shower. The room was set up as a Jack and Jill bathroom, with the door to the master bedroom opposite a door that led to a guest room. That didn't work for them. They wanted the guest-bedroom door to disappear, and they envisioned a new door leading out to an upstairs outdoor deck. Sam told me, "I want a tranquil oasis where I can relax—just come up to my bath with my glass of wine for a soak at the end of a long day." Steve wanted the look of a hardwood floor to complement the floor in their bedroom.

We started by gutting the room. I had Steve and Sam help me remove the vanity, sink, toilet, windows, and wainscoting. Sometimes you just need to clear out bad surfaces and structures, and this type of work, although a little dirty, is really pretty easy and even cathartic. With the room stripped down, we were ready to get on to the fun part of the project.

Although the Garretts' bathroom was sizeable, most of the space was wasted, such as this dead man's corner where a mirror and laundry bag seemed paired almost by accident.

The existing bathroom had a corner sink and vanity that didn't serve the couple well. Everything looked tired. You can see a corner of the brown carpet remnant that covered most of the floor and made for a, well, interesting flooring look.

Steve and I put together the frame for a floating vanity that was going to be mounted on the wall. The frame would support a lot of weight, so we had to make it strong. That meant joining the frame pieces with "biscuits," which are glued into slots in the mated pieces. Reinforced with nailed joints, this type of joinery creates really strong structural frames.

After that, designer Jinnie Choi and I assembled a frame for what would be a long, rectangular, floating (no visible supports) mirror to go over the vanity. We sandwiched and butt-joined pieces of $^3/_4$-inch MDF (medium-density fiberboard), nailing everything in place. We then coated the frame with wood filler to smooth the wood and hide the seams. Once the filler was dry Jinnie sanded it smooth and painted the frame with texture paint. Texture paint comes in many different styles; Jinnie used a tan-colored paint that dries with the appearance of suede.

Meanwhile, carpenter Jake Scott framed out and closed up the guest-bedroom door opening, and framed new openings for the door that would lead to the outside deck and the new window. The room was starting to take shape.

Jake grabbed Sam to work on the new shower that would be placed where the old vanity and sink had been. They installed the

shower pan, and then tiled the wall with travertine stone mosaic tiles. The look was perfect for the natural feel we were after. The tiles come in easy-to-install sheets 12 inches square. Sam was amazed at how simple and quick it was to tile a complete shower surround using these handy sheets.

Meanwhile, I had Steve help me with the facade for the floating vanity. We attached teak boards vertically to create a surface that had a natural elegance and would be the perfect complement to the other natural textures in the room. Teak is a dense, exotic hardwood that is full of natural oils. That makes it a perfect wood to use in an area where water is a near constant.

For the colors in the room, Jinnie decided to go dark and dramatic. She picked brick red for the walls, a color that would work nicely with the wood tones in the space and would perfectly contrast the white fixtures we planned to add. The paint color was also the ideal partner to the new floor Sam and I laid—eco-friendly, tongue-in-groove bamboo strip flooring that had been finished with several layers of charcoal-colored stain. The staining process completely seals the surface and makes the floor largely waterproof.

With the flooring and walls complete, I framed out the supporting structure for the tub. Jake and Steve added teak boards to match what we had done on the front of the vanity. They used varied widths of boards, which gave the surround a much more organic feel. We also installed the vanity, making sure to screw it thoroughly directly into the studs. The vanity was supported entirely by its connection to the wall. A floating vanity leaves floor area exposed, visually increasing the size of the room. This was important because we were using a lot of dark colors and tones in the bathroom, which tend to make a room seem smaller.

The view from the door of the new bathroom, showing the new window and glass door leading to the upstairs deck.

Jinnie lightened the look up a bit with two wall-mounted columns of tiles made from recycled coconut husks. She positioned one running up behind where the mirror unit would go and another behind the bathtub. Add small touches like these for big decorating bang in the minimal space of a bathroom.

I cut the mirror for the custom wall mirror unit, something you can do for your design projects. It's a simple process, but it has to be done carefully. Use a brand new glass

The couple flipped over their new shower enclosure. The seamless glass walls and light stone mosaic tile provide a much-needed counterpoint to all the dark and somber colors in the space.

cutter, dip it in machine oil before each cut, and hold the cutter at a 30-degree angle to the glass. Press down firmly and draw the cutter toward you—you should hear the cutter scoring the glass. Once you have a clear, straight score line, line it up along the edge of the work table, hold the outside edge with a slight downward pressure, and tap the score line from underneath with the ball end of the glass cutter. The glass will break cleanly along the line. We hung the frame on the wall and installed the mirror inside.

A single long "trough" sink takes the place of his-and-hers sinks and makes the space much more usable. The counter looks like slate, but it's actually sandstone that has been rubbed with olive oil. The low-flow toilet is a clear example that eco-friendly solutions can also be some of the most stylish options.

The last step before we'd be able to install the tub and sink was adding a soapstone countertop and tub edge. Soapstone is nonporous, so water won't stain it. Jinnie polished the stone surfaces with olive oil, which creates a reaction that darkens the stone, making it look like slate.

We were finally ready for the fixtures, the biggest of which was the oversized cast iron soaking tub. Getting it up to the second-floor bathroom took some doing, but it looked absolutely perfect once we dropped it in place and added the faucet. The sink was a lot easier, dropping right into the hole we had cut in the top surface of the vanity. Rather than install his-and-hers sinks, we used an unusual option: a long "trough" sink with faucets at either end. Two people can use the sink at the same time, and the look is really cool and unique.

The luxury tub is the perfect place for a long soak, and the surround matches the vanity countertop. Putting the faucet along the side allows anybody taking a bath to comfortably recline either way.

The toilet we installed was also a great look and super eco-friendly. We chose a dual-flush unit that gives you the option of very low flush (0.6 gallon) or a moderate flush (1.6 gallon). It didn't hurt that the design was sleek and elegant. We also saved water by installing a low-flow showerhead.

With the bathtub in the room, we were finally able to install the glass door and window, which Jake did with Steve's help. Once they were finished, I worked with Jake to install the frameless glass shower enclosure. These panels are fitted into tracks on the wall sides and alongside the shower pan, and they are glued together with special clear adhesive on the outside corners. Frameless glass shower enclosures are stunning in any bathroom, and this one proved to be a bright focal point for the Garretts' bathroom.

We added a few final touches, including blinds on the window and door (every bathroom needs to ensure privacy). Then we let the Garretts experience their new master bath. They were stunned and delighted at how the room had turned out. I halfway expected Sam to jump into the bathtub before I could get my crew out of the room!

Color Your Private Enclave

The colors you use in the small space of a bathroom powerfully affect the room's style and feel. Traditionally, bathroom colors have been chosen to reinforce the idea of hygiene. That's why pure white has been—and remains—one of the most popular choices for bathrooms small and large. However, even though the surface areas may be modest, there's a lot you can do with color in a bathroom.

Powder rooms often echo the style of rooms nearby, including the color schemes. Although it's considered risky to use darker colors in small, confined spaces, a half-bath is an exception. Create a dynamic look in your powder room with a deep maroon, dark taupe, or intense gray. Use more muted colors for a less intense look, but one that can be quite elegant. Designers often introduce pattern to spice up what can be a fairly plain room. Bring a bit

Bright white is the perfect counterpoint to a bold bathroom color such as the lime green used here. The white moderates the strength of the color and keeps the room looking fresh and clean. Notice the relief tile on the divider wall. Surfaces such as these add lots of visual interest regardless of color.

YOU CAN . . . Create Stunning Specialized Paint Effects

Paint effects such as rag rolling or sponging look best in small areas, such as an accent wall or the confined space of a powder room. These effects usually involve taking paint off the wall using one material or another—depending on the look you're after. Start with a light base coat in a color that complements others you've used in the home. Then add a noticeably darker or lighter version of the color over the top and, while the top coat is wet, remove sections by rolling a rag over the surface or dabbing it with a sponge (you can also add the top coat using the rag or sponge). Practice first on a large piece of plywood to determine the effect you want. Then go to town on your powder room to create stunningly unique surfaces that will make this small space a big hit.

of excitement to your downstairs bathroom with a colorful, patterned wallpaper, or add other specialty surface coverings such as wainscoting or textured paints to create a sand-covered surface or one that looks like leather.

Most people use lighter, understated hues in a standard detached or guest bath. Work in blues or greens for a calming effect that calls to mind associations of nature and creates a pleasant bathroom environment. The safest way to add a charge to the design is by using a bold color in accent features such as shower- or bath-surround tile, an accent divider wall separating toilet and tub, or in your choice of countertop materials. Keep in mind that you can safely experiment with bolder colors without risking much by simply hanging colored towels. Use reds, oranges, or yellows carefully because warmer hues can close in the space, making it feel claustrophobic and uncomfortable. The same goes for very dark hues, such as dark grays or deep blues. Add bright white on the ceiling and in the trim to effectively "frame" the colors in the space and to give the room a consistently fresh look and feel.

Larger bathrooms are your chance to expand the color palette and be a little adventurous. Sizeable luxury bathrooms can comfortably host more complex color schemes and more color variation throughout the space. However, it's still a bathroom, and the goal usually remains to create a somewhat comforting feeling. Too much color variety or contrast leads to the opposite mood.

I wouldn't hesitate, though, to go dark and dramatic with the color scheme in a larger bathroom (see the Case Study on page 137). In any case, the room should still work visually with the master bedroom if they are directly connected. If the bathroom is a large shared room, you can be a bit more flexible. Always sample

A large bathroom is an ideal opportunity to put interesting colors in play, such as the teal tile columns in this luxury space. However, it's safest to use white as the dominant background hue, as it is here.

both the colors and the surface materials you'll be using in the bathroom, and don't be afraid to change your choices or adjust the colors. The fact is, a bathroom is one of the most heavily used spaces in the home, and it should be attractive at all times.

One caveat I'd offer about the fixtures in any size bathroom: I'd strongly advise you stick to white when replacing or adding tubs, sinks, or toilets. Other colors tend to age very quickly and can create a tired look in a short amount of time. White is classic and works with any color scheme you might dream up for your bathroom.

Illuminating Personal Time

The lighting in a bathroom is as important as the color. Your bathroom lighting has to ensure the safety of people navigating wet surfaces, be bright enough to show dirt and reinforce the notion of cleanliness, and put the best face possible on all the design elements in the room. A lot to ask from simple illumination.

Take your first step to a well-lit bathroom by establishing dispersed overhead lighting. Most bathrooms have an overhead fixture. If yours doesn't, I'd strongly suggest adding one. Evenly dispersed light does a lot for destroying shadows, which are the enemy of any bathroom. Next, you need stronger fill lighting around the tub and shower area.

Dedicated tub or shower lights are a great idea. Smaller bathrooms may not need them if the central light source is strong enough, but good lighting in a bath or shower is a matter of personal safety. If you decide to add a fixture or fixtures in this area, you'll need to be sure the fixture is rated for use in wet environments.

Vanity mirror lighting is one of the biggest flaws in the bathrooms I see on my shows. People often buy over-mirror fixtures that create ugly shadows on faces in the mirror or, worse, they assume a single bright overhead fixture on the ceiling will supply enough light for the vanity mirror. The fact is, the best setup for bathroom mirror lighting is on either side of the mirror. The

You can use lighting decoratively in the bathroom to great effect. In this case, a unique cast glass vanity top has been underlit, creating not only a wonderful visual, but a soft backlight source within the room.

Fixtures positioned on either side of a vanity mirror usually provide the best lighting for a face. Three fixtures are the answer for a pair of sinks, as shown here.

fixtures should be entirely covered—no bare bulbs—and the light should ideally be softly dispersed, not directional. Placing vanity lights on either side of the mirror eliminates shadows when viewing your face in the mirror. This allows you to shave without missing spots, and it will give a woman a truer idea of exactly how her makeup looks. If your mirror is more than 30 inches wide, supplement side lights with a discreet tube light on top of the mirror.

Stylish Sinks and Vanities

Wall-mounted sinks are invariably stylish and increase the visual space of the room but have limited storage. Great for a stylish guest bathroom, but perhaps not the best choice for a high-traffic bathroom where storage is at a premium.

Whether you're redesigning a powder room or a spacious deluxe bathroom, the sink area represents a quick and easy upgrade and a potential spotlight for any bathroom. Swap your tired vanity and sink for a splashy new model and you give the room an overnight facelift. This is also one of the least expensive ways to change the look of the room. Pick a new sink based on the type that best suits your design.

WALL-MOUNTED
These are "floating" sinks, with no part that touches the floor. Wall-mounted sinks are a sleek, contemporary or modern look; the style is usually out of place in a traditional or standard suburban bathroom. A wall-mounted sink generally leaves very little room to place anything on top, and most have no storage capacity. The open space underneath visually makes the room seem bigger.

PEDESTAL
As the name implies, a pedestal sink is supported on a column that hides the plumbing (the sink is usually bolted to the wall, so the pedestal carries very little load). I use pedestal sinks in powder rooms or smaller bathrooms where space is at a premium and storage is not. These sinks are generally an adaptable look that will fit into many design styles, but they don't include storage.

CONSOLE

Console sinks are a lovely look in the right bathroom. The sink rests in a frame with either two or four legs. Most consoles don't include storage, but they often have cross-braces that are great for hanging hand towels. Like pedestals and wall-mounts, console sinks conserve space. You can find this type of sink in many different design styles.

VESSEL

A relatively recent newcomer to the field of bathroom sinks, a vessel sink can have a bowl of hand-painted porcelain, handblown glass, or some other arresting material, such as hammered copper. The drain is usually plumbed down through the counter, and vessel sinks can be used with vanities, thick floating shelves, or other structures and supports—they just need a flat surface on which to sit. The styles are widely varied, but this is a distinctive and unusual look in the bathroom. Make sure you're comfortable with an attention-grabbing feature in the room.

Console sinks are some of the most elegant, especially when backed by a wall of marble tiles!

His-and-hers sinks are a great way to make a master bath much more usable. Vessel sinks create a distinctive style and look great paired with sleek modern faucets, as they are here.

They usually work best in powder rooms, where many people will see them, and the room design can easily be centered around the sink. Be careful when matching a faucet to a vessel sink; the spout has to be low enough to avoid undue splashing.

VANITY SINK

The most traditional approach, vanity sinks can be top-mount (with a visible lip), under-counter mount, or solid-surface (manufactured as part of the vanity counter). The reason vanities and vanity sinks are the most popular style is because of the storage potential the vanity itself offers. Vanities come in all types of materials and styles, and you can vary the look even more by swapping the countertop for a different material.

Traditional bathroom vanities come in a wide range of styles and sizes, and you can even build one to suit your bathroom's space. They are great storage solutions and can add a lot to the style of a room.

FAUCETS

Faucets necessarily go hand-in-glove with a sink, and many bring big style to the party. There's certainly no crime in using a basic faucet (always be sure the handle configuration will match the holes in the counter), but for relatively little expense, you can add a flashy feature to your bathroom design. Chrome is still the most popular and adaptable faucet finish, although you can turn to other finishes for a more unique appearance. Brass, copper, ceramic, and pewter are all options, but I still prefer chrome for its timeless appeal. In any case, match the lines and style of the faucet to your sink and the bathroom at large.

Sumptuous Tubs

Most bathroom redesigns don't involve replacing the tub. It's a big undertaking and can entail significant expense, and it simply may not make sense if the finish on your existing tub is still intact and the space for the tub is limited. But when you want to upgrade the space considerably, a new tub can be a great way to change both the look and the luxury of a bathroom.

The easiest way to update your tub is to swap like with like. Your current tub will be one of two basic styles: built-in or free-standing. Built-in units are either apron alcove (one side showing), corner (two sides showing), or drop in (a lip exposed on top of a custom platform).

Freestanding bathtubs include pedestal units with a solid base, and footed units, like the classic clawfoot tub. Replacing a built-in with a freestanding tub is a fairly easy transition, although the tub location will be limited by where the drain and plumbing pipes run. For ultimate luxury, though, you'll want to consider one of the two types of opulent "experience" tubs: jetted or soaking.

Jetted tubs (often called by the brand names "Whirlpool" or "Jacuzzi") are hugely popular for bathroom remodels. These have powered nozzles built into the body of the tub that swirl the water and create a massaging effect. Most have

A sumptuous tub can make a bathroom infinitely more luxurious. This sleek rectangular unit includes heating, and a wealth of jets to treat your muscles to the ultimate relaxing soak.

A luxury jetted tub can be a stand-alone focal point in a master bath. It can also be a relaxing, indulgent experience like no other. This two-person tub is a perfect example, with custom back rests, molded seats, and multiple adjustable jets.

molded bodies with special forms for reclining and relaxing and include multiple power settings, adjustable nozzles, and special features like lights. They are the height of relaxing spa-like luxury in a bathroom. However, these can run a pretty penny and need to be specially wired and plumbed, and I suggest you be absolutely sure that you'll regularly use the features of the tub so that you get the full worth out of it. Jetted tubs are usually not available as freestanding models, and the motor and jets require a separate platform—so installing one of these requires a lot of space, time, and money.

Soaking tubs are all about taking the bathing experience to new, meditative heights. These are particularly deep units—they range from 2½ to 4 feet deep—that are meant for total submersion. Soaking tubs can be an incredibly restorative experience but here again, if you're not the type to take hour-long baths regularly, the expense may not be worth it. Many soaking tubs are freestanding, so this may be the way to go if you want to add luxury without totally reconfiguring your bathroom.

Super Shower Stalls

A separate shower stall can be a design spotlight that radically changes the look of your bathroom and how you use it. Adding a shower stall in a bathroom with a tub means that two people can bathe at the same time. An independent stall also presents the opportunity to add shower features that wouldn't be possible with a bathtub shower.

There are two ways to find the space for a stand-alone shower stall: Carve it out of existing space in a large bathroom, or replace the tub in smaller quarters. Obviously, it's always better if you can carve the space out of the existing floor plan. (New stalls require at least a 4-foot-square footprint. Any less and the shower will seem cramped and uncomfortable.)

However, I find that when homeowners really think about it, they'll admit that they rarely use the tub for bathing—especially

A frameless shower stall like this one looks super sophisticated in any bathroom. It's convenient and stylish. But it's also an incredible experience with multiple showerheads, including a hand-held version and overhead "rain" showerhead.

a tub in a guest bathroom. Replace a blah tub in a room like this with a showstopping shower stall, and you've upgraded quite a bit without giving up much at all.

When adding a shower stall, you have two options: Build a custom shower stall or install a prefab unit. Installing either type is usually a job for a pro (local building codes strictly regulate how big and what type of shower you can use, temperature regulators on the supply lines, and actual size of the stall and shower pan, among other considerations).

A custom shower stall allows you to include exactly the design elements you want. Create a one-of-a-kind surface with spectacular glass tile in a pattern all your own, add multiple showerheads, or even pipe music into the shower from your main stereo system. The sky's the limit.

This framed corner unit is a prefab shower stall with all the allure of a custom job. The spacious stall includes a steam feature, deluxe adjustable rain showerhead, and a tiled surface that makes taking a shower even more of a pleasure than it normally is.

The great thing about shower stalls is that they can fit just about anywhere. Here, a tiny guest bath features a small-footprint shower stall. It's a practical feature; the design bang is achieved with a stunning mix of mosaic and brick tiles and subtle splashes of style such as the chic faucet and floor vase.

Prefab shower enclosures limit you somewhat in exact size and shape, but they still offer an amazing number of options. Choose from units with built-in seating, steam features, special cavities or ledges for shampoo, soap, and other items, adjustable-height heads, programmable temperature controls, and special lighting features.

Even if you're sticking with your current tub, you can dress it up a bit if you're currently using a shower curtain or low-budget textured sliding doors. Simply adding a new glass tub wall and door can add sparkle and polish to the look of the room. Select from many different textures or plain panels. Frameless designs, in which the glass panels are attached with clip fasteners rather than entire frames, are an especially attractive look.

Spruce up a basic tub-and-shower combo with a deluxe showerhead, sharp-looking tile surround, and neat and trim sliding doors. They sure beat a moldy shower curtain!

Surface Magic

Bathroom surfaces are potential design high points. This is an area of bathroom design where you can add a really stunning feature without doing much damage to your pocketbook. Start with the floor.

Obviously, a bathroom floor needs to be waterproof, but that requirement still leaves a lot of options. The classic choice is ceramic tile. Although basic white tiles remain the most popular, you can pick from a full range of colors. However, be careful when selecting colored tiles for a bathroom. Look for timeless colors and avoid trendy looks. Neutrals are going to be your best bet for a bathroom floor that won't look tired and out-of-date in the short run.

Go sleeker by using glass tiles on your bathroom floor. These are produced with white latex backings so the colors seem luminescent. Glass tiles come in a whole palette of jewel-tone colors that look great as a floor or a half-height tub surround.

Stone mosaic tiles with a decorative row create a fabulous curved tub surround that serves as a focal point in the bathroom. This kind of high-end tile work can set any room apart and, because of the relatively modest surface area, you'll be able to choose a superior material or custom tile without breaking the bank.

Both ceramic and glass tiles come in surface sheens from the common high-gloss to the less popular matte. I usually only use a matte or textured tile surface when slipping on the floor is a big concern. Otherwise, a high-gloss floor surface amplifies the available light and reinforces the sense of cleanliness.

Stone tiles are a good choice for a bathroom featuring other natural textures such as wood. Slip-resistant stones such as slate and soapstone are the best choices for bathroom floors, although polished marble tiles are often used in larger luxury bathrooms. Sealed marble or granite tiles drive home the feel of sumptuous luxury and give you a chance to incorporate amazingly deep and rich colors and patterns into the room's design.

Glass wall tiles are as nice in the bathroom as they are in the kitchen. The tiles come in an incredible number of colors and the surface is easy to keep clean—and just looks fantastic, especially with white fixtures such as this sink and soap holder.

YOU CAN . . . Bring Nature into Your Bathroom

Add an interesting texture to a bathroom floor or the floor of a shower stall with pebble tiles. These are made from smooth river pebbles that are attached to a mesh backing to form foot-square tiles. You lay them as you would sheets of mosaic tiles and walking on them can feel like a foot massage. The look is casual and very natural, a lovely addition to a room with a color scheme of pale greens and blues and wood and glass textures throughout.

Don't feel limited to tiles, though. Sheet linoleum is a great choice for a bathroom, warm and soft underfoot, waterproof, and available in a mind-boggling selection of colors and patterns. It's also a completely natural material, making it an eco-friendly choice.

Sheet vinyl and vinyl tiles offer as impressive a selection of colors and patterns, along with an amazing range of surface textures imitating everything from stones to mosaic tiles. However, I tend to avoid using vinyl because it off-gases volatile organic compounds (VOCs) and creates harmful by-products as it breaks down in the waste stream.

If you're a fan of wood floors—or if you just want to maintain design continuity from an adjacent room into the bathroom—you can re-create the look using bamboo or laminates. You'll need to select those meant specifically for wet environments, but you'll find lots of different stains and grain patterns available.

The floor isn't the only surface you can use to showcase a notable material in a bathroom; the walls are canvases for your creativity as well. Wainscoting is a nice addition to a traditional

The look of dark wood flooring is often a great way to anchor a lighter colored bathroom such as this one. Bamboo and properly sealed hardwoods work fine in a guest bath; higher traffic bathrooms are candidates for laminates with a hardwood surface appearance.

bathroom or a country style. Manufacturers make easy-to-install polyurethane kits that are simpler to work with than wood and more resistant to rot. Tiling walls with the same material you use on the floor is a time-tested way to add elegance to the room. Mix it up and personalize the look by creating a pattern using different shapes of tiles. This takes some planning but can be a truly stunning effect.

A bathroom vanity top or countertop is one of the best places to show off eye-catching colors, materials, and patterns. Solid-surface acrylic or recycled materials work as well in the bathroom as they do in the kitchen. They come in colors from neutral to bold and bright, with patterns ranging from solid colors to flecks and graining imitating the high-quality stone surfaces.

Stone countertops are used less often in the bathroom, and are usually limited to those such as soapstone that are naturally resistant to water and don't need to be regularly sealed. There are so many synthetic bathroom countertop options available now that convincingly mimic the look of stone that the expense and difficulty of working with the real material deters most homeowners.

Bathroom Storage

As in the kitchen, bathroom storage is usually a dynamic part of the room's design (or else it's a missed design opportunity). Here, too, you should store attractive objects in plain sight. For instance, a row of perfume bottles makes a lovely display on a shelf or even on a large vanity countertop.

Start with your towel storage because these are essential in any bathroom. A bathroom with a bathtub or shower must have a place for dry towels and a separate place for wet towels that are in the process of drying. Wet towels draped over shower doors or a bathtub curtain rod give the room a sloppy gym-locker-room look that undermines the room's design. Supplement towel hanging racks with a second set meant just for wet towels, or add hooks to the back of the door, or along a wall in a more casual bathroom, as places for wet towels to dry.

It's always a good idea to store backup towels and washcloths right in the bathroom where they'll be used. Even if you don't have a spacious vanity, you can create attractive towel storage with a wicker basket, or line up folded towels on glass shelves. Keep in mind that the texture and color of your towels (if they're not old and beat up) can add a lot to the room's look.

A divider, such as the dark wood wall here separating the toilet from the bathtub, is the perfect opportunity to add a whole lot of storage to a large bathroom. This divider includes hidden storage in cabinets and lots of shelves for storing in plain sight.

You should also include a modicum of hidden storage in any bathroom for practical items such as toilet paper and cleaning supplies. This can be the under-sink area or a wall-mounted cabinet. Some people use etageres, freestanding cabinets with long legs, meant to straddle the toilet tank. Personally, I find these tend to look flimsy and generally detract from the appearance of a well-designed bathroom. I would much rather see a simple wall-mounted cabinet with sliding doors.

Small Special Touches

Accents and smaller special features can make a big impression in the modest space of most bathrooms. Choose carefully to avoid cluttering the room; the best accents serve a functional as well as an aesthetic role.

Towel warmers are budget-friendly special features that add luxury and a nice form to any bathroom. There are two basic styles: bar and flat-panel. Flat-panel units are often painted in powder-coated enamels (usually white or off-white) and are a more casual,

European look. Bar towel warmers look a bit like chrome ladders. Both styles are available as hardwired or plug-in models and as wall-mounted or freestanding units. Check local building codes, which may specify the placement of electrical features such as towel warmers in relation to tubs or showers. A freestanding towel warmer usually works best in a large bathroom where it won't get in the way of traffic flow. In any case, it will usually be easier and cheaper to use a plug-in model.

Towels themselves are an accent in your bathroom. Although plain white remains a popular choice for all bathrooms, towels in striking colors such as royal blue, deep purple, or tangerine can make a big color statement. Just be sure that the towels you choose don't clash with the bathroom's color scheme. That caveat aside, go wild. You can always replace the towels if the look doesn't do it for you.

Like towels, bath mats are an easy, inexpensive way of adding a splash of color, pattern, or both to the room. Thick, fluffy colorful mats can be a treat for your toes as well as your eyes. You'll also find mats with bright and bold patterns, and even photo

Special features can top off the style of any bathroom, but they often help make the room practical as well. An adjustable magnified shaving mirror in this bathroom helps with close-up cosmetic work, while a handsome rolling blonde-wood caddy provides handy portable storage. The gorgeous shower stall includes two shelves to keep hair care products in order, and an understated bath mat complements the color of the shower tile. It's a very tied-together look.

There's no denying that a marble floor and spectacular tub surround make an impression in the room, but the accents dress it up. Basic black-and-white photos are perfect wall art for this spartan color scheme. The small touches—from the glass cylinder that holds extra soap to the black wicker basket for towels to the personal care product caddies on the tub ledge—serve as the jewelry on a simple and sumptuous bathroom design.

representations of flowers or other designs. Again, like towels, bath mats are so inexpensive and so easily changed that I get adventurous with them.

Candles are a great look in any bathroom. Not only do they create a meditative spa environment when lit, they lend a soft counterpoint to a space usually defined by lines and hard surfaces. There's no need to go overboard, though—a grouping of three pillar candles or a few votives scattered around the room will go a long way toward personalizing the space. Do not allow candles to become clutter that gets in the way of the various functions of the space.

Vanity-top containers are wonderful for accessorizing a bathroom and keeping all the little things you need to store there—from cotton balls to toothbrushes—close at hand. You can buy collections, known as ensembles, from major home retailers, but I like to be a bit more creative than that. Glass apothecary jars, antique bottles, or handmade ceramic containers can all be used as your own custom ensemble. It's yet another way to put your own stamp on the space.

Once you've filled out your bathroom design with these modest elements that help define the look, all that's left is to fill the bath, light a candle, and relax in your newly designed personal spa space.

Candles are some of the most natural accents in any bathroom. They look right at home as decorative elements, and create a relaxing, spa-like feel when lit. Pillar candles are the most common choice for bathrooms, but votives can also serve the room well.

Chapter 6
CHIC GOES OUTDOOR

Creating an outdoor room is not a matter of landscaping. Landscaping focuses on plants, while designing outdoor rooms centers around the way you'll use the space. The plant life

Bring an outdoor room like this together by planning not only the boundaries of the hardscape (here, loose crushed stone), but also by determining the best furniture positioning to take advantage of views and sun exposure.

essentially serves as a varied, enchanting background for entertaining, relaxation, socializing, and fun.

Once more, we'll start with a sketch. This drawing will be your precise road map and is essential, because it's very difficult to judge outdoor spaces accurately just by eyeballing them. Perception can be affected by unusual reference points. Draw the outer boundaries of your yard, and then fill in areas upon which you don't want to encroach, such as a swimming pool, flower garden, or stand of trees. You'll wind up with either a large or a small space for your outdoor room.

For small yard spaces, confine your design to one room or function. You can add small seating areas, but basically you'll want to create one multiuse focal area for your outdoor activities. Choose your outdoor furnishings to make this space as convertible as possible, such as reclining chairs that can be used as sunbathing chaises when you're not socializing.

Break up large yards by putting down hardscape, decking, or soft infill such as tanbark or crushed gravel to create different "rooms" with the yard. Use other features, such as low walls, to define different areas clearly. Dedicate each room to a particular

My team and I managed to get the most out of this small backyard that we redesigned for an episode of *Carter Can*. Although it was a tiny plot of land, we defined a bar-grill area, a separate dining section, and a comfortable relaxation area for rocking and watching the stars.

Bring an intimate dining alcove to life with the same bright color schemes and textures you would use inside. A boldly patterned tablecloth and comfortable and colorful throw pillows and cushions (covered in outdoor weatherproof fabrics) add a huge decorative charge to the small outdoor dining room.

function, such as dining. Ensure continuity by providing pathways from one space to another, but create mystery and visual intrigue by "hiding" different areas out of sight from one another.

In either case, it's going to be a big help if you have a definitive design theme. Regardless of the climate where you live, you can put together your outdoor rooms to suit the experience you want to create. For instance, your home may be located in foothills hundreds of miles from a coast, but that shouldn't stop you if you want to decorate your outdoor space in a beach theme. Identify your theme before you start making any physical changes.

Carter's Case Study:
The White Backyard

Sometimes life gets ahead of you. That's what was happening with Fred and Denise White when I met them. They were getting ready for the arrival of their adopted son, and they desperately wanted their barren backyard to become a place where their son could play and where they could entertain friends. Unfortunately, they'd run a little low on time, energy, and money. If they were going to create the backyard paradise they envisioned, they were going to need to do it Carter's Way.

The existing decorating style in the Whites' backyard could only be described as "desolate."

One end of the yard featured an attempt at landscaping, but the plants were more struggling than thriving.

The "patio" area we found when we arrived featured a tiny black grill that had seen better days and just about zero relief from the sun and the baked soil.

We started by looking at what we had to work with. It was actually a spacious rectangular yard, with a nondescript interlocking concrete block wall surrounding the yard. The Whites' home was located in California's high desert, so the soil was baked hard and there was no plant life to speak of. There was also no shade, and the only sign of life was a feeble grill that had seen better days.

I worked with Fred and Denise to settle on a slightly Caribbean theme that would be airy and attractive. They wanted grass for their son to play on, and we agreed to include three separate areas: a relaxing lounge section, a grilling area, and a separate outdoor dining room.

We decided to use square concrete pavers to define each area. Square pavers are easy to work with and are a relatively inexpensive option, and they clearly define any outdoor room.

Denise and I jumped right into setting the stage for the outdoor lounge. We spread gravel around as a base, and then added a top layer of sand, raking out the surface until it was level. This combination created a stable foundation for the pavers, but also ensured efficient drainage to prevent any water problems. Never just set pavers on the ground, or you'll be faced with an uneven surface in less than a year. The pavers set a nice stage for the open-air pavilion that would feature a large pergola. We continued the pavers into the grilling area and added separate pavers to create a dining area right outside the back door of the house. The layout of the new backyard was now clearly visible.

Designer Jinnie Choi decided to add an interesting counterpoint to all the square pavers. She used molds and a cement mix to create circular pavers of different sizes, which would be used in a pathway connecting the dining room to the pavilion. The circles would also offer some visual relief from all the straight lines in the yard. You can buy stepping stone kits to make your own unique yard additions, and you can even tint them in different colors!

I faced a bit of a challenge in constructing the pergola for the pavilion. The ground in the backyard was simply baked too hard to make anchoring the pergola posts in the soil a practical option. Instead, carpenter Jake Scott and I came up with a good solution. We attached the posts to large planters by drilling a lag bolt through the bottom of the planter into the post. Once we filled the planters with soil, they would be very heavy and stable bases for the posts. It's a solution you can use for arbors, arches, and other garden structures where you don't want to—or can't—anchor the posts in the ground. Just make sure to use water-resistant wood such as pressure-treated pine or cedar.

Setting aside the pergola construction, Fred and I began preparing the backyard walls for a new bamboo fence covering. We attached horizontal pressure-treated 2 x 4 ledgers to the walls using concrete screws. We then screwed the bamboo fence to the

We created this stunning dining area with simple pavers, a little paint, and a section of prefab bamboo screening that's sold by the roll (and that we used on the perimeter wall).

ledgers. The fencing we used comes in rolls (priced by the yard), and is made of complete bamboo stalks for a very natural look. The rolls come in many different colors, but we chose black to give the backyard an intimate, cozy feel. This is a really easy way to add an amazingly attractive border to any yard.

While Fred and Jinnie finished up the fencing, I sketched out a pair of daybeds for the lounge and Jake got to work fabricating them. He used pressure-treated wood for the frame, nailed and glued together, and redwood for the exterior construction. Redwood and cedar are weather-resistant woods that both age to an elegant gray if left untreated. Of course you can also finish them to preserve the natural color, or even stain the wood (although redwood and cedar are so handsome, I would never stain either one).

Jinnie had a great idea for a decorative element that would take the place of plants you would see in a cooler climate. Growing non-native plants in a landscape is usually a mistake because it takes way more resources and time than you should be spending on the landscaping. Instead, Jinnie created several planters full of colorful silk flowers. High-quality silk plants are fairly inexpensive and realistic enough to look convincingly like their living counterparts. Jinnie's designs would provide splashes of color throughout the yard.

Our team had decided to get Fred a badly needed new grill as a yard-warming present. Fred had told us that he loved to talk to his party guests while he was grilling out. So I decided to build him a small dining bar for the front of the grill where guests could sit, eat, and chat. It was a fairly easy project. Jake and I framed it with pressure-treated wood and clad it in redwood all around. I added two steel brackets to support a shallow redwood shelf. We connected the bar to the grill by drilling through the front surface of the grill.

Things were really shaping up, and with all hands on deck, we formed a crew to raise the pergola that would shade the pavilion. We positioned the planter posts in front and back rows of four, attaching a header along each row, joining all the posts in the row. Then we installed joist hangers along the header and nailed the

This luxury lounge space is as beautiful as it is comfortable. Notice the custom pavers that Jinnie whipped up, and the inviting green surface of the synthetic turf.

The custom redwood bar we put on the front of Fred's brand new grill will give guests a great place to sit and shoot the breeze while he cooks up a tasty meal.

cross beams in place. With the planters filled with soil, this construction made for a very stable structure.

It was finally time for the big addition to the yard. Denise had told me she really wanted a lawn, but the arid location meant that a lawn would consume tons of water, creating a big water bill and doing no favors for the environment. Instead we turned to a great alternative: synthetic lawn.

Synthetic lawn surfaces are really gaining in popularity because they are no-maintenance outdoor surfaces that use no water or chemicals such as fertilizer. Unlike the fake turf of years past, today's synthetic grass is an amazingly soft material, and very pleasant to the touch. The process includes compacting a solid level base and then laying the lawn, which is manufactured with a thick rubber backing. Any seams are closed, and chopped up rubber confetti or other soft infill is added over the top, making the surface even softer and helping the synthetic blades stand up and retain their shape. While the lawn was being laid, Jinnie added some additional color by painting random paver squares in reds, oranges, and yellows.

All that was left was to bring in a few nice furnishings, put our custom lounge daybeds in place, hang some sheer outdoor curtains for the pavilion, and set out a few accents. The Whites couldn't believe the transformation, and Denise kicked off her shoes to really enjoy her new "lawn." The couple's new son was going to come home to a very welcoming outdoor space.

Defining Outdoor Rooms

With your theme in mind, begin outlining the outdoor space. Some spaces will be flexible in terms of size or shape—a lounge area or a sunbathing spot can vary greatly depending on how you want to situate it. But other types of spaces, like a dining area or bocce ball court, will necessarily be a certain shape or size.

Once you have the dimensions of your outdoor areas figured out, it's time to choose surfaces to define those areas visually. Start with the outer border.

Your yard, and the areas within it, are most likely bordered by a fence or a wall. Those borders can be a blank canvas on which to start the design of your outdoor room. It's okay to leave a plain fence or brick wall just as is, allowing it to serve as a low-key backdrop to your room design. However, you can also get creative with a yard border just as you might opt for wood paneling instead of a plain painted wall. For instance, if you've chosen a carnival or colorful Caribbean theme, you could paint the boards in a plain wood fence alternating bold colors to add a fun, high-energy visual. If, on the other hand, you're going for a more formal, English country house look, consider lining up a row of hedges in ornate pots along a plain fence to dress it up for your design.

This formal landscape is defined by the layered shrub border, creating a stunning visual backdrop for this outdoor dining room. The central fountain is a lovely touch; outdoor dining is simply nicer next to a water feature.

This outdoor dining room was positioned up against a wall containing a fireplace with wood storage. It's a lovely spot for meals, day or night. The wall helps maintain a sense of intimacy in this outdoor room.

Keep in mind that you can add a more intriguing fence over an existing fence or wall (as we did in this chapter's Case Study, page 165), or create a living wall with a thick row of trees or shrubs.

Inside whatever border you choose, you'll define the exact area of your outdoor room or rooms with one of three basic types of floors: hardscape, decking, or soft surface. Hardscaping is any solid surface such as flagstone slabs, loose gravel or soil, or concrete pavers. Use hardscape for areas that need precise and clear definition, and separations from elements of the architecture. You can also choose a particular hardscape surface just because you like the distinctive look.

There are an amazing number of hardscape paving options from which to choose, but they are all divided into two categories—standardized geometric shapes that are easier to lay, and irregular shapes, such as flagstones, that are more challenging to

A brick patio is the perfect low-key and formal stage for this stunning wicker seating group shaded by a showstopping oversized red umbrella. The hardscape floor gives visitors a solid surface underfoot and a level platform for all the furniture.

DEEP GREEN CHOICES: Paving the Second Time Around

We use a lot of reclaimed wood on my show because it's such an eco-friendly choice and handsome to boot. The same is true of reclaimed pavers. You will find a truly astounding collection of salvaged hardscape materials that can save you money, provide a unique look for your outdoor floors, and give a boost to mother nature. Hundred-year-old brick pavers are often worn smooth and discolored by years of use in city streets. What a cool look for the right yard! Recovered terra cotta patio tiles come in all kinds of shapes and sizes and they, too, have distinctive coloring from years in the sun. Use them for a Mexican or Spanish-themed outdoor room. In any case, you'll find reclaimed pavers at local construction salvage companies. Prices are often negotiable based on how many you intend to buy.

As hardscape surfaces go, sometimes you need to work with what you have. We created this backyard dining area for one of my shows, sprucing up a very plain cement patio. A simple and pleasant dining set centers the outdoor room, and we built bench seating and a "planter wall" to border the room and give it a more intimate and cozy feel. An area rug under the dining table completed the look and softened the appearance of the concrete.

work with but also more visually interesting. Use brick as a simple, traditional, and somewhat formal look for a dining room or party rotunda looking out over your garden. If you're after a high-end look, consider cut slate slabs for an outdoor conversation area next to a hot tub. Granite cobblestones or pavers work wonderfully for a high-traffic area that you want to keep beautiful underfoot.

Wood decking is a classic option for defining outdoor entertaining areas. The problem I have with decking for an outdoor room is that it tends to set the area apart, because most decks are elevated. However, you can run a low deck right into a grassy expanse or over a hardscaped floor to create a more seamless look. Regardless of the height, integrate the "room" created by

YOU CAN . . . Lay a "Deck" by Yourself

Elevated decks require structural reinforcement and complex construction. You can, however, lay a wood deck surface on ground level and avoid the trouble of building a substructure. Deck tiles are the way to do it. These are tiles made from wood that has been attached to a waterproof plastic backing. The backing ensures that there is drainage away from the wood, preventing rot. These plastic base "trays" have ears on them that allow them to be connected together. You simply clear and level an area as you would for any paver, set the tiles in position, and click them together to create a lovely wood surface in a few hours. Manufacturers offer many different surface designs such as herringbone or simpler straight-board looks. Laying a wood deck in this way takes very little time, expertise, tools, or effort, and it's a perfect way to define an outdoor room.

An attractive outdoor wood floor like this can be laid in a few hours, and the surface designs available include the plain tiles used in the field of this floor and the fancier look of the border tiles.

The plastic tile bases securely hold the wood surface in place while allowing drainage to prevent any moisture-related problems. The tiles have discreet ears on all sides for securing to adjacent tiles.

The simplest look in deck tiles—a four-board pattern that can be rotated to create a regular pattern in the surface of the outdoor floor.

I don't usually position outdoor rooms on grass because traffic can beat up even a healthy lawn. However, the lawn can be an ideal setting for a dining room that sees occasional use. Recreation takes place elsewhere in the yard, and this room is perfect for barefoot dining . . . no spill cleanup required!

a deck into the yard at large by including multiple entry points (usually stairs), adding container plants on the deck itself, and designing the deck to be detached from the house as much as possible.

The last outdoor room flooring option is grass. Although grass might seem like the natural choice, it isn't the ideal surface for an outdoor room. Grass is expensive, requires a great deal of maintenance, uses a lot of water, and can be easily damaged where there is a lot of foot traffic (such as a busy social outdoor room used for entertaining!). That's why I prefer to use wood or hardscape. If you choose grass for your outdoor room, pick the hardiest variety of sod available in your area, and keep it cut slightly lower than normal.

Furnishing the Outdoor Room

Define your outdoor room and set down a good, solid floor, and you're ready to furnish the place. Just as you would in an interior room, you'll make choices between keeping your existing outdoor furniture and buying or making new. Outdoor furniture understandably ages more quickly than its indoor counterparts, given the exposure to the elements and hard use in season.

DINING TABLES

Outdoor dining table options are plentiful, and the material you choose is really a matter of taste. Wood, such as a teak set, is a very natural addition to an outdoor room, one that will emphasize the connection to plants in your landscape. However, many types of wood furniture require yearly maintenance to ensure they last as long as possible. I would suggest paying a bit more for redwood, cedar, or an oily hardwood such as teak or tigerwood—you'll probably save money in the long run because the furniture will inevitably last longer.

Metal outdoor dining tables and chairs are extremely popular, especially tables with glass tops. Even painted and coated metals are prone to rust if exposed to wet conditions over time, but metal outdoor furniture, by and large, will last a good long time. The most common colors are black, white, and brown, but nothing's stopping you from repainting a metal table and chairs in brighter colors to suit a particular design style. More important,

Use matching furniture to tie different outdoor rooms together, as the homeowner has done here. If you choose wrought iron furnishings like these, include plush cushions like the ones shown here to make the furniture more comfortable and add changeable color elements.

Where the sun exposure is direct and intense, an oversized umbrella ensures that you can linger outdoors as long as you like without getting sunburned. This table comes with a stylish stone top, a great feature for an outdoor surface.

closely inspect any fabric portions of metal furniture. Synthetics last much longer than natural fibers such as cotton. Any fabric is going to wear over time, but really, they are much more comfortable and inviting than a pure metal seating surface.

A dining table is a natural partner next to a pool so that adults can eat and watch kids swim, or swimmers can jump out for a bite or a drink at a pool party. This iron set includes comfortable fabric seats and backs that ensure everyone is cool and relaxed even when the day heats up.

CASUAL SEATING

Use outdoor chairs and chaises to create inviting social or relaxation areas. Use the same guidelines for furniture spacing and placement that I provided in chapter 4 (page 95). Casual seating can be arranged as a conversational grouping in a larger outdoor room, or as a grouping centered around a focal point, such as a water feature or sunset. If you choose to include bench seating, I'd strongly suggest that you use a bench with a back; backless benches can be uncomfortable for some people.

The look of this furniture group is sophisticated, but the pieces are also very durable, crafted in resin wicker. The cushions are covered in outdoor fabric, and the umbrella stand is specially designed not to fall over. Consider both the practical and aesthetic in choosing furniture for your outdoor rooms, and combine the two whenever possible.

This backyard needed a special look, which is what my team and I gave it with a detailed arbor including built-in seating and a separate decorative structure. The structures create different areas—for dining, relaxing around a fire pit, or mingling during a party—and the overhead joists provide broken shade and support for decorative accents such as the glass bead post decoration and a wind-and-sun shade.

If you've selected a high-end design theme, you can find furniture to go there with you—including sectional couches and large, comfortable easy chairs. Manufacturers make incredible weather-resistant treated wicker furniture in sophisticated styles, and faux leather versions as well. These are constructed with finishes, cushions, and fabrics that hold up to sun, water, and heavy use. They are great ways to establish your style and truly create an outdoor room. In addition to seating, you'll find companion tables, ottomans, and other furniture.

STAND-ALONE STRUCTURES

Certain stand-alone structures are unique to outdoor rooms, and include pergolas, arbors, archways, and combinations that offer seating or built-in trellises. These types of structures serve both decorative—they are inevitably graceful and beautiful—and practical purposes. You can train any number of climbing plants to grow over a pergola or arbor, and the structure provides modest broken shade for seating underneath. The designs of these structures can be complex or simple, and you can build them from scratch or buy kits. Wood is the traditional material, but newer composite materials or synthetics such as polyurethane are durable, light, easy to work with, and often less expensive than wood. When I include this type of structure for an outdoor room, I either want to reinforce the dimensions of the room, cover the entire area with the structure, or use a more modest structure as a portal to another area such a lawn or garden path.

As stand-alone structures go, it's hard to top a pavilion. These are often equipped—as this one has been—with curtains and fabric roof. (You can do the same to an arbor to create a similar effect.) The complete package creates a separate and nearly private lounge area.

Let There Be Shade

Sun and rain are part of the reality of any outdoor room. Rain usually sends people indoors, but harsh, bright sun can do the same—it can be just too much of a good thing. A shade feature can make any outdoor room much more comfortable and, depending on the one you choose, more stylish as well.

UMBRELLAS

Use an umbrella as a local and portable shade solution. Whether I'm adding an umbrella to an outdoor dining table or using one to shade a lounge area, I always look for an adjustable model. The more adaptable the umbrella, the more usable it will be. If you're putting together your outdoor room in high style, you can find incredibly posh freestanding umbrella units with scintillating, curvaceous forms.

SHADE SAILS AND SHADE CLOTHS

A shade sail is a piece of synthetic or natural cloth with grommets that slip over eye hooks attaching the sail to the house and/or overhanging structures. These can be quite dramatic statements in

Shade cloths can be woven through overhang structures such as the beams over this outdoor room, creating a three-season space, with lovely filtered light and graceful shapes overhead.

their own right. I find they work best as a roof to a modern or contemporary outdoor room. They are more work than an umbrella and not as portable, but because they come in different shapes—often triangular—they add lots of visual interest. You'll also find shade sails in many different colors and even patterns, adding yet another facet to their design potential. Shade cloths are generally sections of fabric such as canvas or treated cotton that are interwoven through the cross beams of an arbor or other structure, shading the area below. A shade cloth can be a great way to make a lounge area more comfortable in all kinds of weather.

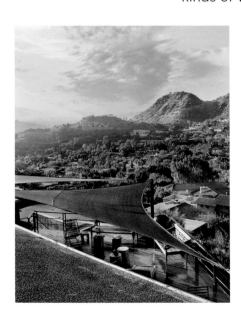

Shade sails can be dramatic shapes, like birds frozen in mid flight. The shade they cast, and the forms overhead, add flair to any outdoor room, and the sails themselves come in different colors.

AWNINGS

I'm not a fan of awnings, but they are functional shade structures. They are usually limited to areas next to the house because most have to be mounted onto a wall of the house. They come in both hand-operated and motorized versions, and more expensive styles are offered in a moderate range of colors. To my eye, though, the awning has to complement the architecture of the house, look good in context of the outdoor room style that you've established, and shade the area you need shaded exactly when you need the shade. That's a lot to ask from a fixed feature such as an awning.

If your yard is large, you may need to incorporate multiple shade features. But I would recommend using them only where you actually want and need shade; they are usually a little pricey and ineffective to serve as decorative features on their own.

Accenting the Outdoor Room

As with every room in the house, much of the personality of an outdoor room comes from the decorative features you add. There are many to choose from, but your choice should be driven by

A self-supporting hammock adds a wonderful form and decorative element to outdoor rooms, and is a great place to relax and enjoy the landscape and the sun.

the style you've already chosen for your outdoor room. In addition, no decorative feature should interfere with the function of an outdoor room.

Sculptural accents include simple concrete or ceramic animals, orbs, and other decorations. Used within the borders of your outdoor room, this type of decoration can be completely unique, or you can carry through a theme established elsewhere in the landscaping by incorporating the same elements used in a garden or along a path. I find that less is always more when it comes to outdoor room statuary and sculpture, and restraint is the better part of style. Much as we may all love lawn gnomes or cute ceramic frogs playing the guitar, those are the velvet paintings of an outdoor room.

Classic accents such as amillaries (iron sculptures of a globe shape with an arrow through it), sundials, and gazing balls are all attractive additions to most any outdoor room. Decorative urns are also common additions to an outdoor room, and you can find them in many different finishes—from glazes to distressed terra cotta—to complement your outdoor furnishings. Groupings of three different sized urns are some of the most attractive and popular decorations in an outdoor room.

A simple birdbath is a relatively inexpensive and easy decorative element to add to your outdoor room, whether you put it in the middle of a hardscape surface or use it as a focal point among adjacent plantings.

Water features are more rare in an outdoor room setting. Ponds and waterfalls are outside the discussion of exterior room decoration because they are really landscaping features. If there is already a pond in your yard, look to position your outdoor room nearby to take advantage of the view and sound of running water, if any. A fountain or birdbath can be a nice touch for a large social area or a pavilion meant for relaxing. Fountains come small to large, tiered and one-level, freestanding and wall-mounted. Pick one that suits the size of your outdoor room and a style that appeals to your design sense. Stick to plug-in models rather than hardwired versions. This will make adding the feature easier and will give you the option of moving it as you see fit. Birdbaths are static and can be put just about anywhere in an outdoor room. Keep in mind, though, that birds can actually be messy, and they draw other wildlife to the area.

Potted plants are natural partners to an outdoor room design. Not only do the containers that you choose provide you with unique decorative options, you can select plants that reinforce the lines, textures, and colors you've chosen to use in your outdoor room. It's also a lovely way to maintain a sense of continuity from the garden into the outdoor recreation or relaxation space.

Taming Fire

A grill is invariably a wonderful addition to any outdoor space, but it's not the only use for flame in your exterior rooms. Fire pits and fireplaces can be spectacular additions to an outdoor room, and they can even serve as centerpieces for those rooms.

Fire pits are the easiest feature to add into the layout of an outdoor room because they're portable and the prices range from incredibly affordable to incredibly pricey. The differences between the low end and the high end are materials, design, and extra features. At both ends of the scale, there is a mind-boggling number of pit designs available. Choices also vary by fuel source. Gel fuel fire pits are self-contained and don't leave ash, making them cleaner than traditional wood-burning pits. You can also buy gas fire pits powered by propane.

The most basic fire pit—a good choice if you are just creating a small seating area for nighttime stargazing—is a simple steel bowl with basic legs or a base and a dome-shaped screen to go over the top. A high-end model—more appropriate for a large, luxury yard, an outdoor sectional sofa, and other luxury features—may include ledges for food and drink around the outside of the pit;

A fire pit just seems to draw people in, and a high-style version such as this one, with its deep copper lip, will keep visitors lounging around the fire on long summer nights and chillier fall evenings alike.

specialized materials such as hammered copper, cut stone, or a combination; and a complete cover in addition to a screen, which allows you to safely close the fire pit once you go inside for the night.

The size of your fire pit should correspond to the size of your furniture grouping, because the idea is to warm every possible seat in the outdoor room.

You can make a fire pit fairly easily, as we did for this backyard. We used a metal liner and created a fireproof lip for the pit with broken pieces of flagstone. It's a great, informal look. Paver pathways connect the fire pit area with all the other outdoor rooms in the yard.

Outdoor fireplaces are available in a similar range of styles and prices. Custom-building one is out of the DIY realm for most homeowners, but you can buy large outdoor fireplace units or easy-to-assemble kits. These look almost as stylish as a completely custom-built unit and can be placed anywhere in an outdoor room. Smaller gas or electric fireplaces can be used almost as decorative accents rather than focal points.

Chimineas are a style unto themselves, and look like miniature potbelly woodburning stoves. They too can be placed anywhere on an outdoor hardscape surface, but the look is usually out of place with a contemporary or modern outdoor room design.

Light the Nighttime Yard

No outdoor room should be closed off simply because the sun goes down. There are a vast number of lighting solutions that will make your outdoor room as enjoyable after dark as it is under the glare of the sun.

General ambient lighting is going to provide some level of nighttime illumination for your outdoor space. Light from house-mounted safety fixtures and the glow from windows will provide a small amount of light for outdoor rooms close to the house. However, you'll most likely need to supplement those light sources.

The most desirable outdoor lighting is directed from the waist down. This creates a safe environment for moving around

An umbrella post-mounted light provides soft, dispersed illumination perfect for an outdoor meal at night without breaking the spell of the dusky dark beyond your outdoor room.

and leaves the night sky open and undiluted, creating a sense of spaciousness. However, some theme lighting, like tiki torches or lighting in overhangs such as an arbor or porch extension, can create the feel of an actual room. Strong lighting such as this is appropriate if you'll be playing board games or prepping and cooking a meal after dark, or if a large party of people will be interacting.

DEEP GREEN CHOICES: Plugging into the Sun

Perhaps the biggest challenge in effectively lighting an outdoor space is wiring in the fixtures. You can alleviate a lot of the headaches of running underground conduit or aboveground weatherproof wiring by using solar outdoor lights. These come equipped with small batteries that are charged by solar panels designed into the fixtures. After the sun goes down, the fixture automatically lights up, and stays that way until the sun rises again. Although most solar lights are not super bright, use enough of them and you can light most of your outdoor space without wiring in a fixture. The fixtures also come in many different styles and finishes, so it's easy to find one that blends right into your outdoor decor.

Of course, outdoor lighting doesn't necessarily have to be all about function. Uplights positioned to highlight a dramatic specimen planting or part of the home's architecture can add big visual impact to the view from an outdoor room at night. You can even install waterproof fixtures in a pond to light the water feature from inside out and create a unique look next to your outdoor room.

No matter what type of lighting you choose, always light pathways, steps, the edges of an outdoor room, and points of access and egress including pool ladders and house doors.

The beautiful thing about an outdoor room is that the surroundings continually change and, in turn, change the look of the room. Establish an outdoor room design that suits your style and pleases your eye, and it will seem fresh for a long time to come.

Torches such as these are an elegant and wonderful way to light the perimeter of an outdoor room. Flame is a more natural look than electric light, and the soft, dispersed illumination lends a romantic feel to any outdoor room at night.

Bringing It All Together

Once you've got your outdoor rooms in shape, your house should be looking pretty great! Just the same, styles change over time. New products are introduced, new colors hit the market, and more important, you own tastes evolve. Someone once said that nothing is constant but change. That couldn't be more true than in the world of home decorating and remodeling.

Although the idea that almost every design has an expiration date might seem like a downer, it's actually not. In fact, part of the excitement of putting your own unique stamp on your home's design is the fact that the design should always be evolving. It's fun to surprise friends and family who walk in only to notice some great new feature you've introduced to a room—whether it's a whole new suite of furnishings or just a different arrangment of pictures on a wall.

Experimenting is part of Carter's Way, and experimenting with your home design never stops. As long as you're having fun, it's all good. So I hope you'll keep this book on hand and turn to it when you want to revisit the design of a particular room or the whole darn house. That's why I wrote it, and I hope it continues to serve you well.

RESOURCES

AMERICAN SOCIETY OF INTERIOR DESIGNERS
When the project is a little too big for you to manage, or you need outside help for any reason, turn to ASID-certified designers.
www.asid.org

BENJAMIN MOORE NO-VOC PAINT
This longstanding manufacturer of interior paints offers no-VOC versions under the Ben and Natura lines.
www.benjaminmoore.com

ENERGY STAR PROGRAM
Find information on saving energy in your home as well as the lowdown on Energy Star–rated appliances at this consumer site.
www.energystar.gov

FOREST STEWARDSHIP COUNCIL (FSC)
Nonprofit advocate of sustainable and responsible forest management practices. Look for the council's seal any time you shop for lumber to ensure the wood was harvested in an ecologically responsible way.
www.fsc.org

GLOBAL GREEN USA
Global Green is the American division of the Green Cross, working toward the organization's mission of creating a "sustainable and secure future by reconnecting humanity with the environment."
www.globalgreen.org

GREEN AMERICA: ECONOMIC ACTION FOR A JUST PLANET
A social activism site, Green America offers information on a wide range of topics including green living issues that affect homeowners.
www.greenamericatoday.org

HABITAT FOR HUMANITY RESTORES
Nonprofit retail outlets selling reclaimed building materials for use in new home designs.
www.habitat.org/restores

HEALTH HOUSE
A website of the American Lung Association dedicated to providing information on indoor air quality and building and design practices that affect that quality.
www.healthhouse.org

HGTV
For projects from my shows, show schedules, clips, and insightful articles on different home decorating and remodeling topics, visit the channel's website.
www.hgtv.com/carter-can/show/index.html

NARI GREEN
The sustainable practices arm of the National Association of the Remodeling Industry. Provides information for contractors and homeowners regarding sustainable remodeling practices and materials.
www.greenremodeling.org

NATIONAL KITCHEN & BATH ASSOCIATION
Find remodeling professionals, design ideas, and many other resources for your new kitchen or bathroom design at this comprehensive industry and consumer website.
www.nkba.org

OLYMPIC PAINTS
This manufacturer offers a no-VOC premium paint.
www.olympic.com/Paint/Go_Green

SHERWIN-WILLIAMS
The paint company sells no-VOC versions under the ProMar label.
www.sherwin-williams.com/pro/green

SOLAR LIVING INSTITUTE
This nonprofit provides an amazing amount of information about using solar power in the home, solar issues, and much more.
www.solarliving.org

US DEPARTMENT OF ENERGY, ENERGY EFFICIENCY AND RENEWABLE ENERGY INFORMATION CENTER

This government resource provides a wealth of information on eco-friendly energy technologies and practices for everyone, including homeowners, to tap.

www1.eere.energy.gov/informationcenter

THE US GREEN BUILDING COUNCIL

A clearinghouse for information about green building practice and the LEEDs (Leadership in Energy and Environmental Design) certification program.

www.usgbc.org

YOLO COLORHOUSE

This paint manufacturer is one of a handful of companies producing no-VOC, low odor paint—a key factor in minimizing home remodeling impact on indoor air quality. Fantastic colors as well!

www.yolocolorhouse.com

PHOTO CREDITS

Pg. 93: Photo courtesy of Maxwood Furniture, www.maxtrixkids.com; Pg. 94: Photo courtesy of Mirage, www.miragefloors.com, (800) 463-1303; Pgs. 96-97: Photos courtesy of Mohawk Flooring, www.mohawkflooring.com, (800)-266-4295; Pg. 98: Photo courtesy of Sitcom Furniture, www.sitcomfurniture.com, (510) 434-1600; Pg. 99: © 2012, HGTV/Scripps Networks, LLC. All Rights Reserved; Pg. 100: Photo courtesy of Mirage, www.miragefloors.com, (800) 463-1303; Pg. 101: Photo courtesy of Mohawk Flooring, www.mohawkflooring.com, (800)-266-4295; Pg. 102: Photo courtesy of HomerWood, homerwood.com, (814) 827-3855; Pgs. 103-05, 107-08: © 2012, HGTV/Scripps Networks, LLC. All Rights Reserved; Pgs. 109-11: Photos courtesy of Hooker Furniture, www.hookerfurniture.com, (276) 656-3335; Pg. 113: Photo courtesy of Crossville, Inc., CrossvilleInc.com, (931) 484-2110; Pg. 114: Photos courtesy of ClosetMaid, www.closetmaid.com, (800) 874-0008; Pg. 116: Photo courtesy of Mohawk Flooring, www.mohawkflooring.com, (800)-266-4295; Pg. 117: Photo courtesy of CalicoCorners, www.calicocorners.com, (800) 213-6366; Pg. 118: Photo courtesy of HomerWood, homerwood.com, (814) 827-3855; Pg. 119: Photo courtesy of Mirage, www.miragefloors.com, (800) 463-1303; Pg. 120: Photo courtesy of HomerWood, homerwood.com, (814) 827-3855; Pg. 121: Photo courtesy of American Lighting, www.americanlighting.com; Pg. 122: Photo courtesy of HomerWood, homerwood.com, (814) 827-3855; Pg. 123: Photo courtesy of Flor, Inc., www.flor.com, (866) 281-3567; Pg. 124: (top) Photo courtesy of Hooker Furniture, www.hookerfurniture.com, (276) 656-3335; (bottom) Photo courtesy of Anji Mountain, www.anjimountain.com; Pg. 125: Photo courtesy of Sitcom Furniture, www.sitcomfurniture.com, (510) 434-1600; Pg. 126: Photo courtesy of CalicoCorners, www.calicocorners.com, (800) 213-6366; Pg. 127: Photo courtesy of VivaTerra, www.vivaterra.com, (800) 233-6011; Pg. 128: Photo courtesy of Crossville, Inc., CrossvilleInc.com, (931) 484-2110; Pg. 129: Photo courtesy of CalicoCorners, www.calicocorners.com, (800) 213-6366; Pg. 130: Photo courtesy of Mirage, www.miragefloors.com, (800) 463-1303; Pg. 132: © 2012, HGTV/Scripps Networks, LLC. All Rights Reserved; Pg. 133: Photo courtesy of Crossville, Inc., CrossvilleInc.com, (931) 484-2110; Pg. 134: Photo courtesy of Green Mountain Soapstone, www.greenmountainsoapstone.com, (800) 585-5636; Pg. 135: Photo courtesy of Mr. Steam, www.mrsteam.com, (800) 72-STEAM; Pg. 136: Photo courtesy of Alumax, www.alumaxshowerdoor.com, (800) 643-1514; Pgs. 137-41: © 2012, HGTV/Scripps Networks, LLC. All Rights Reserved; Pg. 142: Photo courtesy of TOTO USA, Inc., www.totousa.com, (888) 295-8134; Pg. 144: Photo courtesy Merillat, www.merillat.com; Pg. 145: (top) Photo courtesy of American Lighting, www.americanlighting.com; (bottom) Photo courtesy Merillat, www.merillat.com; Pg. 146: Photo courtesy of Vigo Industries LLC, www.vigoindustries.com, (866) 591-7792; Pg. 147: (top) Photo courtesy of Kallista, www.kallista.com, (888) 452-5547; (bottom) Photo courtesy of Crossville, Inc., CrossvilleInc.com, (931) 484-2110; Pg. 148: Photo courtesy of TOTO USA, Inc., www.totousa.com, (888) 295-8134; Pg. 149: Photo courtesy of American Standard, www.americanstandard-us.com. (800) 442-1902; Pg. 150: Photo courtesy of Jacuzzi® Luxury Bath, www.jacuzzi.com, (800) 288-4002; Pg. 151: Photo courtesy of Mr. Steam, www.mrsteam.com, (800) 72-STEAM; Pgs. 152-53: Photos courtesy of Alumax, www.alumaxshowerdoor.com, (800) 643-1514; Pg. 154: Photo courtesy of Crossville, Inc., CrossvilleInc.com, (931) 484-2110; Pg. 155: (top) Photos courtesy of Interstyle Ceramic & Glass, www.interstyle.ca, (604) 421-7229; (bottom) Photo courtesy of Stratastones, www.stratastones.net, (800) 807-1549; Pg. 156 and 158: Photos courtesy of TOTO USA, Inc., www.totousa.com, (888) 295-8134; Pg. 159: Photo courtesy of Alumax, www.alumaxshowerdoor.com, (800) 643-1514; Pg. 160: Photo courtesy of American Standard, www.americanstandard-us.com. (800) 442-1902; Pg. 161: (top) Photo courtesy of American Standard, www.americanstandard-us.com. (800) 442-1902; (bottom) Photo by Suki Medencevic; courtesy of DeWitt Designer Kitchens, www.dewittdesignerkitchens.com, (626) 792-8833; Pg. 162: Photo courtesy of Frontgate, www.frontgate.com, (888) 263-9850; Pg. 163: © 2012, HGTV/Scripps Networks, LLC. All Rights Reserved; Pg. 164: (top) Photo courtesy of CalicoCorners, www.calicocorners.com, (800) 213-6366; (bottom) © 2012, HGTV/Scripps Networks, LLC. All Rights Reserved; Pgs. 165-70: © 2012, HGTV/Scripps Networks, LLC. All Rights Reserved; Pgs. 171-72: Photos courtesy of Frontgate, www.frontgate.com, (888) 263-9850; Pg. 173: Photo courtesy of The Chair King, www.chairking.com, (800) 829-9955; Pg. 174: © 2012, HGTV/Scripps Networks, LLC. All Rights Reserved; Pg. 175: Photos courtesy of HandyDeck, www.handydeck.com, (866) 206-8316; Pg. 176: Photo courtesy of The Chair King, www.chairking.com, (800) 829-9955; Pg. 177: Photo courtesy of CalicoCorners, www.calicocorners.com, (800) 213-6366; Pg. 178: Photo courtesy of Frontgate, www.frontgate.com, (888) 263-9850; Pg. 179: Photos courtesy of The Chair King, www.chairking.com, (800) 829-9955; Pg. 180: © 2012, HGTV/Scripps Networks, LLC. All Rights Reserved; Pg. 181: Photo courtesy of Frontgate, www.frontgate.com, (888) 263-9850; Pg. 182: Photos courtesy of Tenshon, www.tenshon.com, (480) 663-3166; Pgs. 183-84, 186: Photos courtesy of Frontgate, www.frontgate.com, (888) 263-9850; Pg. 187: © 2012, HGTV/Scripps Networks, LLC. All Rights Reserved; Pgs. 188-89: Photos courtesy of Frontgate, www.frontgate.com, (888) 263-9850; Pg. 190: © 2012, HGTV/Scripps Networks, LLC. All Rights Reserved.

ACKNOWLEDGMENTS

To my beautiful wife Amy, for putting up with all of the long days and nights in order to get the information I needed to complete this book, and for giving me the inspiration to conquer every day after. Thanks to my Mom and Dad, for giving me the strength and will to be the person that I am today and giving me three great siblings, and thanks to Todd, Tyler and Sienna in their own right for always being there. Thanks to Rachael Ray for promoting the DIYers in every field, and writing the foreword to my book. I'd like to thank Robert Flutie, who has helped steer the CO ship day in and day out. To Chris Peterson, for blending my thoughts and words in a concise manner. And last but not least, to Frank Belcastro, Jinnie Choi, and Jake Scott for providing the much-needed manpower to complete every project you see in this book.

ABOUT THE AUTHORS

Carter Oosterhouse started out as a model and actor, keeping bread on the table with his carpentry work, including behind-the-scenes work for home improvement shows on The Learning Channel. In 2003, he landed a part as a cast member of TLC's series *Trading Spaces.* In 2007, he was offered the chance to host his own show, *Carter Can,* on HGTV. Based on the success of that show, he was tapped in 2008 to co-host *Red, Hot & Green* with Nicole Facciuto. He has also been a contributor to the *Today Show* as "America's Handyman," and he regularly appears on *The Rachael Ray Show, The Tyra Banks Show,* and other programs as both a home improvement expert and an authority on green home design, materials, and practices. He's been featured in a number of magazines, including being named *People* magazine's "sexiest man on television" and included on their list of "sexiest men alive." He is also the face of Nautica's Voyage fragrance for men. He's very involved in charitable work for children's causes, including projects with New York's Books for Kids Foundation, COACH (Community Outreach Assistance for Children's Health), Boys and Girls Clubs of America, and the Hole in the Wall Gang Camp. In 2008, he started Carter's Kids, a foundation dedicated to building safe and fun playgrounds in disadvantaged neighborhoods throughout the county. He has his own website, websites for his shows on HGTV's website, a Facebook account, and a Twitter page.

Chris Peterson has written extensively on the subject of home improvement and home design. A list of his work can be found at petersonink.com.